CHOICES ARE NOT CHILD'S PLAY

Helping Your Kids Make Wise Decisions

CHOICES ARE NOT CHILD'S PLAY

Helping Your Kids Make Wise Decisions

Pat Holt
Grace Ketterman, M.D.

Harold Shaw Publishers
Wheaton, Illinois

for Dave,
the best choice of all

ISBN 0-87788-117-0

Cover design: Greg Clark

Library of Congress Cataloging-in-Publication Data

Holt, Pat, 1943-
    Choices are not child's play : helping your kids make wise decisions / Pat Holt and Grace Ketterman.
        p. cm.
    Includes bibliographical references.
    ISBN 0-87788-117-0
    1. Decision-making in children. 2. Child rearing.
    I. Ketterman, Grace H. II. Title.
    BF723.D34H64 1990
    649'.7—dc20   90-32453
                                                    CIP

99 98 97 96 95 94 93 92 91 90

10 9 8 7 6 5 4 3 2 1

Contents

Contents

Acknowledgments

Years ago, Barbara Streisand vocally assured us that "People who need people are the luckiest people in the world." We are most fortunate because in writing *Choices Are Not Child's Play*, we needed many people.

Jennifer Hoadley, a gifted teen-age poet, came up with the title so quickly that we were awed by her ability.

Rigoberto Reyes, a trusted friend, located important statistics that no one else could find—and we'd tried numerous sources.

Nancy Barshaw, Linda Coyle, Eunice Dirks, Kathy Enos, Dale and Cindy Hindman, and **Sally Kneser** were invaluable sources of information and experience.

Liz George, Cheryl Langley, and **Trudi Ponder** gave the greatest gift of all—the gift of time in prayer for our writing.

A last word of gratitude to our dynamic agent, **Joyce Farrell,** to our angel editor **Ramona Cramer Tucker,** and to the people at Harold Shaw Publishers. They chose us and have responsibly accepted the consequences with kindness and generosity.

Two roads diverged in a wood, and I—.
I took the one less traveled by,
And that has made all the difference.
ROBERT FROST

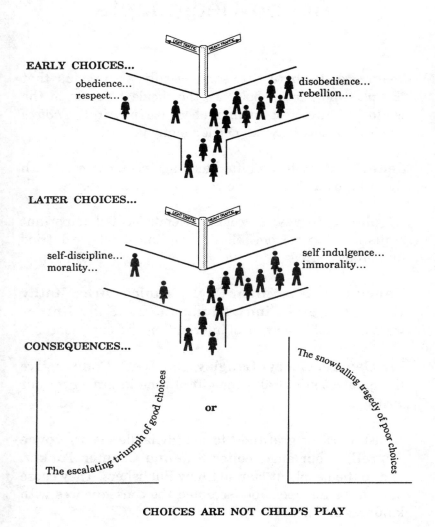

EARLY CHOICES...

obedience...
respect...

disobedience...
rebellion...

LATER CHOICES...

self-discipline...
morality...

self indulgence...
immorality...

CONSEQUENCES...

The escalating triumph of good choices

or

The snowballing tragedy of poor choices

CHOICES ARE NOT CHILD'S PLAY

Introduction

A good laugh is sunshine in a house.
THACKERY

New parents typically envision a home where laughter is heard often and enjoyed by the entire family. They dream of a home free from the problems of their personal backgrounds. But all too soon the magnitude of parental responsibility adds a sobering touch of reality to the dream family. New parents sigh, "We had no idea such a little one would take so much time, energy, and money!"

No matter the responsibilities and struggles of parenting, moms and dads find joy in their new roles as parents. With each sweet gurgle, dimply smile, kicking of wee feet, and grasping of tiny fists, parental excitement is renewed.

These parents dream big dreams for their child. Carefully cuddling a newborn infant, parents think of the precious new life as President, CEO, Pulitzer or Nobel Prize winner, world famous athlete, etc. It is incomprehensible that parents would dream of rearing that delightful baby to become an addict, a terrorist, a thief, a drug peddler, or a prostitute.

Family life seems to take one of two directions as the years go by. The parental experience either becomes more enriching with greater opportunities for shared laughter and enjoyment with children, or it becomes a series of disappointments. We know several parents who have referred to parenthood as "the longest and most encumbering 'have-to' in all of life." For families that wind up in the latter track, laughter is an infrequent visitor in their homes.

In Sidney Sheldon's popular novel *Rage of Angels,* the heroine captures the feeling of ultimate frustration:

> *There came a sudden burst of merriment, and it was such an alien sound that she stopped for a moment to listen . . . looking into the past, trying to understand when it was that all the laughter died.*[1]

Far too often, parents throw up helpless hands, feeling defeated and defenseless against the far-reaching consequences of their children's choices—the choices of the children they have nurtured, loved, protected, and provided for to the best of their abilities. When does the parental laughter die, and why?

The death of family joy and parental satisfaction does not happen suddenly with one poor choice; it usually comes so gradually that uninformed or less alert parents could let the signs slip past unnoticed.

The old frog example holds true. Put a frog into scalding water, and he will jump around, desperate to escape. Put another in cold water over a steadily increasing flame, the frog will kick back to enjoy his warm bath until he's completely cooked! Because the change happens so gradually to Frog #2, he does not notice or react to the imminent peril—and the result is disaster.

Many parents take after Frog #2. They do not sense the far-reaching implications of the abundance of poor choices their children are making—until it is too late.

Choices Are Not Child's Play will encourage parents at each stage of their child's development. From our own experience as parents, as well as from our professional experience as medical doctor, child psychiatrist, educator, and educational consultant, we believe that children can be guided into patterns of wise decision-making. Providing a child with limited, age-appropriate choices, allowing the child to make his or her own decision from the choices provided, and permitting the child to assume responsibility for the consequences of each choice from the earliest age can teach a child to make responsible choices, to accept outcomes of personal choices, and to make increasingly better choices as a result.

Parents and their children can become confident, self-controlled, and mutually respecting. Our vision is an ever-increasing number of homes filled with the sunshine of laughter!

Pat Holt
Grace Ketterman, M.D.

Part I

What's Happening to Our Children

*Destiny is not a matter of chance;
it is a matter of choice.*
AUTHOR UNKNOWN

– 1 –
It's a
Different
World

The theme song from a popular TV show enthusiastically proclaims, "It's a different world than where you've come from. . . ." Parents sigh deeply and remark, "It certainly is!"

While some elements of parenting are timeless, most have changed considerably since the days when today's parents were children. And if you go back a decade or two further, the lifestyle differences are dramatic.

Just how different is family life for children today than for a child of the long-ago 1930s? Compare the major transitions in lifestyle between the 1930s and 1980s on the following page.

Major Transitions in Lifestyle[1]

Characteristics	Norm 1930	Norm 1980
Family interaction	high	low
Value system	homogeneous	heterogeneous
Role models	consonant	dissonant
Logical consequences	experienced	avoided
Intergenerational associations	many	few
Education	less	more
Level of information	low	high
Technology	low	high
Non-negotiable tasks	many	few
Family work	much	little
Family size	large	small
Family type	extended	nuclear
Step/Blended/Single-parent families	few	many
Class Size (K-12)	18-22	28-35
Neighborhood schools	dominant	rare

Some of the comparisons in this chart reflect societal trends that are easily recognizable. There have been many years of high-tech industrialization since the days when families worked together on farms or in family businesses. Today's couples generally choose to have fewer children, and diverse family structures abound—stepfamilies, blended families, and single-parent families. A family's choices are as diverse as the contemporary smorgasbord of lifestyle choices for the individual.

School Days

The 1930s and 40s was an era of strong family interaction and inherent stability, combined with a value system that all of society recognized. That stable value system is reflected in the junior- and senior-high schools of the 1940s. The leading school problems in that decade were:

Talking
Chewing gum
Making noise
Running in the hallways
Getting out of place in line
Wearing improper clothing
Not putting paper in wastebaskets

One teacher recalls his high-school teaching career in the late 1940s with great fondness:

The young people, for the most part, wanted to learn and came to school eager for what I would teach. I was proud to be a teacher and was treated with great respect by the students and their parents. I remember catching a boy chewing gum. He was embarrassed, apologized, and assured me that it would not happen again. I smiled and told him I'd keep the matter between the two of us. He was pleased with that. What the teachers said counted. The students knew it, and they knew that their parents would back us up 100 percent.

Doesn't it sound almost ludicrous today to call such simple, innocent, somewhat insignificant issues "problems"? Today's educators would have a completely different list of concerns:

Drug abuse
Alcohol abuse
Pregnancy
Suicide
Rape
Robbery
Assault
Burglary
Arson
Shootings
Bombings[2]

A recent ex-teacher shared his experience of teaching junior high:

I went to college for five years to fulfill my childhood dream of becoming a teacher. I wanted to make a difference in the lives of the students of today. Reality hit on the first day, as I looked into the faces of children whose youth was already long gone. They were hardened, and it became painfully obvious they had seen, heard, and experienced far more than I hoped I ever would. Still I hung on to my dream, but their complete lack of respect, their open rebellion to authority, their total lack of motivation to learn dented my dream on a daily basis. The lack of parental support to the point of negligence in combination with students who resented any attempts to build responsibility or self-control shattered my dream. I left the pieces and found another profession.

This teacher's experience poses quite a contrast to that of the teacher from the 1940s. The changes are dramatic. Sadly, today's world of the 90s truly is "a different world than where we've come from."

Peer Pressure

In this very "different world" children experience tremendous peer pressure and greater opportunity to make choices—the kinds of choices that could bring an early and lifelong harvest of healthy relationships, or disaster.

Peer pressure starts early. Even a young child is highly aware of his peers. Day-care workers have discovered that it is much easier to potty-train two two-year-olds at once, than one at a time. Seeing a young friend toilet-train encourages another child to try it also. A five or six-year-old may want to learn how to tie his shoelaces because he's seen a friend attempt it.

As your child grows older, he or she faces increasing peer pressure. When all her friends have Cabbage Patch Kids, your eight-year-old wants one too. When your seven-year old's friends have Nintendo and Teenage Mutant Ninja Turtles, you can guess what he wants for Christmas.

Then in a few years, your child is bombarded with a whole new set of peer pressures: when to wear makeup, the type of clothes to wear (of course they have to keep up with the latest name brand), even the way to talk. "The group" becomes so important that your child would do almost anything to remain a part of it.

The highly esteemed founders of the Gesell Institute of Child Development tell us that the enthusiasm of a twelve-year-old "can be so strong that the child is carried away by it. . . . The group is indeed very important to the twelve-year-old. His own identity can become lost within the group."[3]

This enthusiasm coupled with a desire for group acceptance can lead to good choices or to the poor choices that can put even a young child on the pathway to self-destruction.

What pressures do our children face today? Let's look at a few of them.

Self-Esteem Roller Coaster

"You're ugly."
"You can't do anything right."
"What a klutz!"

No matter how old they are, your children may hear one or more of these phrases, or ones like them, every day. An eight-year old may be chosen last for a baseball team because everybody else on his team knows he can't hit a ball to save his life. An adolescent may endure teasing about her complexion or figure. A teen may feel ugly, unwanted, because no one has asked her to go to the spring banquet.

If a child feels rejected by his peers early in life, he may feel a lack of self-esteem (the "I can't measure up" feeling) for the rest of his life. This feeling of worthlessness, added to the normal, emotional ups and downs of teen life, can easily lead to suicide attempts, withdrawal from family and peers, resentment, hostility, or violence.

Crime

Even young children risk being excluded from the in-group if they don't agree with the group's standards.

Because of this pressure to be part of the group, the number of petty and violent crimes is rising. Elementary-school children are encouraged to steal, lie, or cheat on tests to prove their worth to friends. Teens in high school may be pressured to have sex, use drugs, or rob a store to prove their passage into a gang. Even school staff have been reported to encourage cheating in order to raise scholastic scores.

Concerned parents believe that violence among youth has reached intolerable levels. The homicide statistics are chilling. In 1986, four to five people under age 18 were murdered per day, ten percent more than in 1985. Equally horrifying, three to four people under 18 were arrested for murder every day, a seven percent increase over 1985.

Teens are twice as likely as adults to be victims of violent crime and ten times more likely than the elderly. Even more disturbing, 45 percent of teen victims reported that they recognized the offender.[4]

Sexual Pressure

Sexual pressure begins early. Junior-high boys (and younger) are encouraged to "go all the way" on dates in order to prove their virility; junior-high girls are told they are frigid—or worse—if they don't make out with every guy they date. Because sexual relationships run rampant in high schools, sexually transmitted diseases (STD's) and pregnancies are reaching alarming proportions.

Unfortunately, the television, movie, and secular music industries—for the most part—fail to portray the consequences, the dark side of illicit sex. What teens see is the happy-go-lucky, into-one-bed-and-out-into-another, no-strings-attached relationships.

And sexual activity isn't the only thing that television and movies promote.

Drug & Alcohol Abuse

Why do students take drugs? A 1987 *Weekly Reader* survey found that television and movies had the greatest influence on fourth- through sixth-graders in making drugs and alcohol seem attractive. The second greatest influence was other children. Children in grades four through six think that the most important reason for alcohol and marijuana is to "fit in with others," followed closely by a desire "to feel older."

These elementary-school-age children are not just *experiencing* peer pressure; an ever-increasing number of them succumb to try drugs and alcohol. Just take a look at this chart.

Percentage of 6th Graders Who Report Peer Pressure to Try Drugs[5]

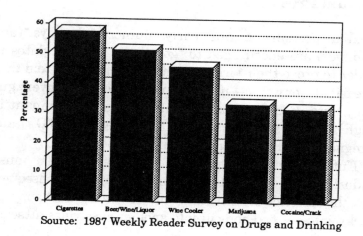

Source: 1987 Weekly Reader Survey on Drugs and Drinking

Jerry was nine years old when he came to his new school. He longed to be popular and to fit in with the kids, but he felt embarrassed because he was the shortest boy in the class. To escape the teasing and taunting, Jerry proved he was really "big." He told the other kids he had a big brother who showed him how to smoke "pot" and that he had a couple of beers every weekend. At first the other children didn't believe him, but two or three visits to Jerry's home convinced them he was telling the truth. With Jerry's leading, several others in the class also tried pot and beer.

Jerry's story is repeated more often than we like to believe! Since 1975, the percentage of students using drugs by the sixth grade has *tripled.* In the early 1960s, marijuana use was virtually nonexistent among thirteen-year-olds, but today one in six thirteen-year-olds has used marijuana. Forty-two percent of sixth-graders and 26 percent of fourth-graders (ages nine-ten) have used alcohol.[6]

In the United States, the choice to experiment with drugs accelerates at an alarming rate through the school grades, earning our nation a dubious distinction. We have the highest rate of teenage drug use of any nation in the industrialized world. Statistics from the National Institute on Drug Abuse, provided in the chart on the next page, confirm this appalling trend.[7]

The drug problem affects *all* types of students—from the streets of the city to the tree-lined sidewalks of the suburbs. Escape from the city does not insure a drug-free adolescence as this mother can confirm:

I wanted the best for my children. I knew the junior-high school and high school in our city had a drug problem, so I thought the best thing would be to move away. Even though it meant my husband and I had to leave higher-

paying jobs, we moved to a rural area for the sake of our children. It didn't take long to find that the rural schools had the same problems as the city schools. Only the numbers of people involved were different. When I found out my teenager had been experimenting with drugs, that was it. We packed up and came back to the city. Now, at least, I expect the problem, know what to look for, and have people to help my husband and me deal with our children.

Lifetime Prevalence for Selected Drugs Among 8th, 10th, and 12th Grade Students* 1987

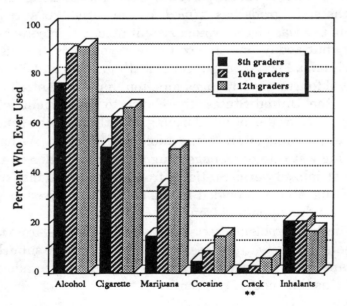

* Data on 8th and 10th grade students is from the *National Adolescent Student Health Survey.* Data on 12th graders is from the *High School Senior Survey.*

** Reflects a subset of any use of cocaine.

Our children are besieged with opportunities to purchase and use drugs at school. And drug suppliers have responded to that increasing demand by developing new strains, producing reprocessed, purified drugs, and using underground laboratories to create more powerful forms of illegal drugs. Consequently, users are exposed to heightened or unknown levels of risk. Drug-related emergency room episodes and deaths show a frightening rise of ruinous consequences: debilitation of mind, body, and emotions; severe medical and social consequences; family upheaval that reverberates through years of agony.

The statistics are staggering. The evidence is overwhelming. Far too many young people have slid "a long way, baby" in this very "different world." Each of them have chosen to "do it my way," and all are living with regret!

Choosing in Today's World

The widespread availability and number of choices young people face is startling. It isn't just a limited few "bad" kids who are exposed to the lure of drugs and drinking, sexual activity, crime, or the up-and-down battle with self-esteem. All kids—from young adults to teens—are given the option.

The conclusion is obvious: ***Parents of this generation must commit themselves to the difficult, but not impossible task of guiding their children to make wise decisions, and allowing them to assume the responsibility for these decisions to attain the quality of life we all seek.***

In the pages that follow, we'll explore the needs that influence children's choices, not just in regard to using drugs, but in all areas of choice.

– 2 –
Your Child's Needs

Sixteen-year-old Nate sat glumly beside my desk. His blond hair was well cut and carefully groomed; his preppy clothes fit well and were obviously clean and pressed. His face, sadly set, did not match. It alternately expressed anger, cynicism, and, rarely, a touch of good humor. When I (Grace) asked him what he was proud of, in all of his life, he fell silent.

After a long pause, Nate commented, "All I'm good at is having fun!" He was failing in school, he and his parents fought regularly, and he could not recall completing a single project for months, if ever. Nate was depressed—a prime candidate for some major acts of rebellion.

What exactly was wrong with Nate? It took me hours to root out some underlying emotions that were causing Nate's problems. One of the things I discovered was that, though his parents loved him, they had failed to meet some of his basic needs as a child and adolescent. Because of this, Nate had never really felt loved.

Basic Needs

What do we mean by basic needs? Dr. William Glasser believes that children have five basic needs:

- *Physical needs*—food, clothing, and shelter

- *The need to belong*—acceptance, recognition, affection

- *Power*—the ability to make and carry out some decisions and plans

- *Freedom*—within a well-defined and maintained set of elastic boundaries

- *Fun*—the opportunity at work or play to find enjoyment, laughter, and fulfillment[1]

Another recognized authority lists three primary emotional needs of children:

- *Unconditional acceptance*

- *Approval*

- *Consistency*[2]

We would add a fourth, and very important, need to his list—the need for humor—a chance to laugh in even the most tense situations.

A third category of need definition grows from the world of Dr. Eric Berne. In his memorable book, *Games People Play*,[3] Dr. Berne clearly shows that everyone needs what he calls "strokes." Strokes are ways of giving attention, and all children are good at getting strokes by crying (early on), being charming (later on), or misbehaving (still later on). They prefer loving, protective, and understanding strokes that are given freely (the unconditional, positive type), but they quickly learn to gain strokes (the conditional, positive kind) through hard work, by doing many of the things adults ask or expect.

When parents overlook these efforts or don't recognize their importance, children may feel stroke-deprived. Without realizing what they are doing, they begin to misbehave because they are disappointed or frustrated. All too often, children find they can get more intense and prompt attention from parents by wrong actions than they did by being good and charming. So little children start to throw tantrums in front of your company or stage screaming fits at the grocery store. Older children may "talk back" or run away from home—anything to draw attention to themselves.

When parents don't fulfill a child's need in a loving way, the child will strive more and more intensely to get that need met in any way at all, *even negatively.*

When Needs Are Not Met

When basic needs are not met, children become anxious and fearful. Like Linda, they may think, "Mommy spends so much time with the baby, maybe she doesn't love me anymore!" When Dad insists the lights go out at bedtime, Jimmy is likely to wonder: "What if a monster comes in my room and I can't see him?" Or Jill, who is four, thinks, "It's not fair! I have to take a nap and John (seven) never has to!"

We could go on and on with the list of children's fears, worries, and anger. You could probably come up with quite a few yourself! But many children fail to put such powerful feelings into words. Instead, they tend to act them out in distorted ways. Linda is far more likely to whine, get into her mother's makeup, or torment the baby than she is to say simply, "Mommy, I'm lonely and sad when you don't seem to have time for me." And Jimmy, who really wants to be brave to earn Dad's approval, may bang on his wall or break his toys to prove how strong he is. Little Jill might just kick and scream when Mom makes her take a nap.

Since the best of parents often don't know why their children are misbehaving, they react by scolding or punishing. Naturally, these parents don't want their children to be selfish, cowardly, or overly aggressive.

Act, Don't React

Understanding how behaviors and emotions connect with fundamental needs is vital for teaching choices to your children. The very earliest choices include proper responses to needs and feelings. Rather than reacting to a need by misbehaving, your child can learn to:

- Define and verbalize feelings

- Find out what need has created this feeling as well as what is needed to heal the painful emotion

- Discover to whom to go and how to seek the help that is so needed

Behavioral psychologists have wonderful tools for helping to eliminate annoying actions. For basically secure children, these tools are often enough.

Behavioral change methods fall short, however, when they fail to recognize the deep undercurrent of needs and emotions within the heart of a child. So, all too often, children and parents stumble along, doing the very best they can—falling frequently into dark and dangerous paths of misunderstanding and lack of knowledge. Instead of *acting*, they *react* to one another.

As a parent, you need to gain a clear perspective of issues and form plans that are certain to meet needs, thereby guiding your children into healthy life patterns. Such thoughtful parenting can help your child develop wisdom and learn to make smart choices all throughout his life.

In the next chapter, we'll discuss how your child's needs change as he grows.

– 3 –
From Birth to Young Adult

An expert in children's mental health once stated, "Good mental health is the ability to make smart decisions." Decisions are choices learned very early in life. They begin with the decision to express a need (hunger or discomfort of any sort), accept its fulfillment, respond with trust (and eventually love), and grow into a healthy adult. Obviously, infants do not "choose" to cry when they are uncomfortable, or cuddle and coo when they feel good. These are, quite frankly, physical reflexes.

However, these early, simple, reflex actions impact parents powerfully. And whether parents know it or not, they *do* have choices that monumentally influence their babies. They can react to their crying child with calmness, comfort, and protection, thus teaching trust and providing security. They can respond in frustration and anger (even abuse), offering the slim security that the child is not being abandoned, but creating pain and anxiety. Or they can ignore the needy child, creating a climate where there is no bonding of child to parent, no security at all. The child is left with anger over the continuing pain, wondering if he will ever receive a response to his outcries.

Choices are clearly *not* child's play! They originate in your response to your infant's simple needs for food, comfort, and shelter. The way you nurse your child, provide warm, dry clothing, and whether you cuddle and rock your baby can make all the difference in the world to that child now—and later.

Early Choices

As your child begins to grow, you must decide how much and how far you will let her explore her world. Where can Mindy safely crawl, and what can Bobby taste and feel in his tiny environment? Wise parents encourage the decision to explore but balance that permission with the establishment of a protective environment. They are always present in that environment to teach their growing child to choose wisely.

When your child is twelve months of age, take time to teach him or her to choose to obey in order to avoid danger. Perhaps the first wise choice any child really makes is learned through pain. That pain may be Mom's or Dad's persistent removal and firm "No!" when Junior begins to touch a breakable object or taste a dangerous chemical like bleach or detergent. Or the learning experience may be a blistered finger that brushes a hot iron or stove.

As your child's language develops, his ability to reason and choose becomes more extensive and complex. What Christopher wants for breakfast or what Hilary would like to wear today can be wonderful opportunities for learning decision-making. Or they can explode into power struggles that make both parent and child angry or anxious.

Early choices are highly self-centered; they are based on your child's physical needs. As you respond, you also recognize your child's need for belonging, some degree of personal power, and growing desire for freedom, all mixed with the happy ingredient of fun.

Your Growing, Changing Child

As your child matures, he will have different types of needs. Let's take a look at what they are, grouped by age.

Birth to two

We've already discussed the primary needs in these months: food, warmth, and shelter. The regular cuddling, along with nourishment, soft sounds, and the glow of your loving eyes lay the cornerstone of security. Your choice to be patient, tender, strong, gentle, and consistent in your response will enable your infant to cry out his or her needs confidently. A harsh, angry response will rarely stop a child's crying out, and it fails to develop a sense of safety and trust. Instead, it encourages nervousness and fear. However, failing to respond at all, or so slowly that your child gives up, is the most damaging decision of all.

Needs of Children, Birth to Two

- *Food*
- *Warmth*
- *Shelter*

In these months, your child begins to crawl, walk, taste, and explore every part of her world. She needs freedom and some degree of power. When you, as a parent, take delight in such explorations yet provide protection against dangerous risks, her trust in you grows—and so does her ability to enjoy her world.

Two to three

The "Terrible Twos" are an extremely important time in your child's life, although they can be tremendously frustrating to you. Many books have been written about how to cope during this stage. But what many researchers and writers fail to recognize is the immensity of the change that the two-year-olds themselves must endure! These toddlers move from almost total care by parents to a great amount of self-care. They feed themselves, begin to use the toilet, entertain themselves, give up bottle- or breast-feeding (if they haven't already), and often engage in combat with a brother or sister.

Needs of Two- to Three-Year-Olds

- *Power*
- *Freedom*
- *Independence*
- *Security*

Your two- or three-year-old wants to be independent (the need for freedom and power), but she is also afraid of giving up the physical closeness and the assurance of belonging she has felt. Discovering that you are present even when she is not touching you—and that you will still respond to her needs, is a major task for her. You'll discover that when you are consistently there, your child will relax and make fewer demands. Satisfying that need for balance in freedom and restraints is quite a challenge for you!

Three to five

Preschoolers are capable of so many choices, it's amazing! And that's a blessing, because they have so many to make. The needs for power, freedom, and fun are abundant and quite easy to meet. The need for boundaries in which to explore freedom and power *safely* is a paradox, but is easy to understand.

Preschoolers love to create and imagine. They would just as soon color walls as a coloring book. They could track an imaginary creature to the horizon, never minding the possibility of getting lost. If you failed to set some limits, your preschooler would never take a nap and would collapse from exhaustion.

Needs of Three- to Five-Year Olds

- *Freedom*
- *Power*
- *Limits*
- *Fun*
- *Discipline and training*

So those universal needs demand your wise guidance and limits. Within those limits, your preschooler can decide what to wear, which crayons to use, what books to love, and even which playmates to choose. He won't always choose to take turns, to be obedient, or to follow the rules. So his need for power and freedom must be balanced with his need for discipline and training. To merit the approval they need, children must learn to give up some of their freedom in order to grant others a fair share of space and privilege.

A special word about the needs of four-year-olds. Universally, Fours are full of questions. The "Why?"s, "How?"s, and "How come?"s are matched only by the "Where?"s and "Who?"s. You may become apoplectic after carefully explaining how the baby kittens were born only to hear Marty ask, for the tenth time, "But where did they come from?"

At four, there is a remarkable need for satisfying curiosity and acquiring information. Fours build these new needs on top of the old needs to belong and to feel important! So in discovering a new depth of attention from parents' efforts to explain, a four-year-old will keep on asking. It works! She not only gains the facts she seeks, but, in addition, she experiences the first glimpses of hope that she will one day enter your adult world.

In these days of widespread use of substitute care, parents face a unique challenge. If you really want to teach the rudiments of decision making to your child, don't leave too much to the preschool or day-care staff and be especially selective in choosing caregivers! They do the best they can, but there is no way they can effectively offer each child the individual time, attention, and basic focusing-in that are needed.

Plan the time you do have with your preschooler to zero in on asking questions, exploring sources of answers, and sticking with the process until the need is satisfied. As preschoolers ask and explore, they learn and discover. Accurate knowledge is the basis of smart choices. So even if learning simple facts seems to have no direct relationship to decision making, remember how vital the facts really are. Take time to teach your preschooler about life!

Elementary school (5–12)

The needs of five- to twelve-year-olds are even more extensive than in earlier times of development. At this time, your child must develop a sense of responsibility. He will have to practice advanced social graces in teamwork and cooperation as well as in constructive competition. How she chooses to master the academic, social, and physical skills will indeed determine her destiny.

Needs of Elementary-School-Age Children

- *To be responsible*
- *To be capable in at least one area*
- *To believe in his / her own worth*
- *To master social, academic, physical skills*
- *To balance personal freedom with parental limits*

Every child needs to be a star! In order to believe in her worth, your child must have tangible evidence that she is capable in at least one area. If your school doesn't practice the philosophy of discovering, developing, and demonstrating each child's unique gifts, encourage teachers and administrators to do this. If possible, find a teacher or school that does focus on the gifts of individual children.

While your control over a school system is limited, your own input into your child's self-discovery can be unlimited. Try out your child's interest and ability in art, music, sports, and mechanics. Expose your son to a variety of people who can share their jobs, hobbies, and creative skills. Involve your daughter in creative projects, seeing to it that she completes her work and showing your pride in her efforts and the results. Telling someone else about the project will help your child believe in her worth.

Wait a minute. What does self-esteem building have to do with choices? *Everything!* The child who has solid evidence that he is worth something will have what it takes to master good decision-making skills.

Remember Nate, whose only asset was the ability to have fun? His ability to choose to go to college will never materialize unless he chooses to study, to defer pleasure, to earn money, and to assume basic responsibilities. He doesn't have any evidence of ability, competence, or past successes on which to base new choices. Therefore, it's easier for him to stay front-runner in the fun games of life than to risk being mediocre or poor at something else. If he doesn't try, he can't fail. And he can always believe that he could succeed, if he had only wanted to try! Nate's decision making is tragically limited.

Because Nate has a long-term power struggle with his parents, his choices are restricted further. His mother nags at him about studying and tells him how much better his grades would be if only he didn't spend class time writing notes or doodling. He disagrees. He feels he doesn't waste time and vows that he only needs to study before a test. Furthermore, if he begins to change his habits now, Nate believes it will mean that Mom has been right all along. What self-respecting young male rebel (or any teenager for that matter) can afford to make such a concession?

Nate is at grave risk. His friends are more than likely to influence him to choose destructively. Why not skip school?

Why not choose to feel good—drugs will help, and so will excitement of any kind! Nate's life is a sad example of the disastrous decisions promoted by power struggles between family members.

All school-age children need to succeed at something. Your child needs to experience affirmation and encouragement. He must learn that he can try and fail, without despairing. He needs enough freedom from you in which to explore and grow but enough parental limits to prevent foolish choices with disastrous results.

Your school-age child needs to belong to a select group besides your family that values him and within which he can feel comfortable. But he needs your help in asserting his independence and individuality in order to avoid submission to negative authorities or peer pressures.

If you have built a good relationship with your child, you will be able to help him fulfill his needs. As a parent, you'll need plenty of love, time, clear thinking, and excellent communications skills. You'll need to sort through your own values and beliefs, and you may even have to give up some TV time to think and read in order to reach some of your own conclusions. Your child's needs must merit not only your consideration, but your actions!

Adolescence (12–18)

Like it or not, most decisions made by your adolescent will be made quite independently of you.

In a way, adolescents repeat the two-year-old's struggle for independence. Only this time it's for keeps! A two-year-old settles into development and leaves behind the frustrating tantrums over limits and desires. The adolescent, however, moves into the full responsibility of adulthood all too soon. And when the earlier needs have not been met successfully, the shaky foundation will cause immense problems in the superstructure.

It's easy for parents to panic during the adolescent years. All too often they re-parent (treat an adolescent like a two-year-old), or they try a get-tough approach that results in their child's rebellion. Instead, invite your adolescent into the adult world with coaching and gentle, but strong, guidance.

Needs of Adolescents

- *To explore and to collect information*
- *Parental confidence and a sounding-board*
- *A balance of personal freedom and protective parenting*
- *Time with peers*
- *Emotional distance from parents*
- *Criteria by which to distinguish right from wrong*
- *Increasing opportunities actually to make decisions*

What needs do adolescents have? Your adolescent needs a chance to explore the world and to collect information that will lead to good, independent decision making. She needs you to give her clear criteria by which to distinguish right from wrong, establish values, and discover how to adapt these to her own lifestyle. (No longer is your parental authority, alone, a wise outline for adolescent behavior! Your adolescent needs to learn how to think on her own.)

Your adolescent needs you to trust her in this new area of freedom. She needs wide enough separation from you to experience independence without hurt feelings or anger.

(This is especially important if your adolescent has felt close or dependent on you. It's *not* intended to offend you!) But she doesn't need to be left entirely on her own. A balance in personal freedom and protective parenting will prevent any really serious mistakes.

Every adolescent needs time enough with peers to develop a sense of belonging to a group. But she also needs guidance to discover and value her own identity as uniquely different from that group. You can help by being a sounding board. Listen without being shocked, and respond with good sense—without lecturing. In addition, expect the best from your adolescent.

Young adults (18–25)

Whether they attend college or enter the job force, young adults have their own special set of challenges and needs.

Because our Western culture forces young people to grow up too soon, young adults are likely to have a poor foundation for decision making. Often, they have had too little adult feedback and too much freedom. They often lack the capability to learn from past experiences and tend to keep testing authority figures in an unconscious effort to get someone to set some logical limits on them—and care enough to enforce them.

On the other hand, many young adults act as if they believe life can go on forever in the semi-adult twilight zone of overly-emancipated adolescence. They seek pleasure without an adequate sense of responsibility and with unrealistic expectations. This can result in a rootlessness that offers no security and little sense of achievement and personal worth. They are highly vulnerable to depression and are likely to seek relief and excitement in drugs or alcohol.

Needs of Young Adults

- *A basic understanding of right and wrong*
- *Clear guidelines and expectations*
- *Parental support and encouragement,
  balanced with limits*
- *A chance to struggle with difficult situations*
- *Logical feedback and the chance to process choices*

What your young adult needs is easily understood but difficult to provide. Legally she has independence and, practically speaking, no one can force her to function in a prescribed manner. (You may be nodding your head emphatically; you've tried force, and you know it doesn't work!) Only breaking the law can provide meaningful consequences. And even that extreme is often handled in a manner that lets young adults get by without learning basic lessons.

Young adults need a basic understanding of right and wrong and some philosophy regarding *why* something is wrong or right—a well-developed sense of morality. They need a chance to struggle with difficult situations, to learn from mistakes, and to find opportunities to start over and improve.

How can you help? Give your young adult support and encouragement, balanced with clear limits as to how far your help extends. Young adults need clear guidelines and expectations on the job and in school or training. The consequences for failing to measure up must be equally clear and consistently enforced.

Help for All Ages

Knowing the basic needs of children of all ages—and the emotions that are woven into them—is paramount to realizing how choices are made. Understanding this important connection will help you guide your children in the serious business of making wise decisions.

In the next chapter, we'll look at ways you can remove any obstacles to good decision making.

– 4 –
Obstacles to Good Choices

"**I** really don't *want* to go to college. What if I flunk out or something?" Nate's low self-esteem echoed off the walls of my office and into my heart.

In spite of everything his parents, teachers, and counselors had done to help him, Nate still was not able to make the choices that he needed to make as a young adult. He was a depressed underachiever whose future options were seriously limited by his inability to cope.

Why couldn't Nate make wise choices? There are seven hindrances to wise decision making that affect not only Nate, but ourselves, and our children.

Reaction to Events

When your child is an infant or a toddler, it is abundantly clear that you react to your child's needs (your child cries and you pick him up). Your child, in turn, responds to your reaction (he cuddles close to you and smiles); then you respond to his reaction (you smile back at him), etc. While some of this cycle is instinctive, it can, on the other hand, set up a pattern that omits the function of intellect.

All too often, we, as parents, limit an entire category of choices to *reaction*. Reactive decisions often occur when emotions are at peak levels. For example, your children Dennis (two) and Eva (four) fight over toys. When Dennis grabs the ball and refuses to share it (typical of a two-year-old), Eva is inevitably going to attempt to wrest it out of his grip and keep it. Their choices are based on power and fun. Eva wants to keep the ball (that feeling of power!) in order to have fun (as each defines it). They forget, of course, that they would have *more* fun by sharing it. And they don't even think well enough yet to realize they are seeking power by competing for possession. They operate strongly on an instinctive level.

The very foundation stones for building good choice-making skills rests with you, the parent or caregiver. If you count up the times you have reacted too much like Dennis and Eva, you may feel embarrassed. While we as adults may not want possession of the ball for our fun, many of us play out this scenario:

> *Mom, tired of the kids' fighting and wanting them to play together "nicely" yells, "You two stop fighting and yelling or I'll take that ball away from both of you!"*
>
>   *Since no self-respecting child can give in too easily, the struggle continues. Trying to follow through, Mom stops her activity, goes over and grabs the ball, and places it on top of the refrigerator. The results? Now the children are angry at each other and at Mom and are likely to*

restrict their next fight to a place away from Mom's hearing.

This mom may *feel* powerful because the present battle has stopped, but no one really learns any valuable lessons. How much better it would have been for that mom to take a few minutes to think about the life-lessons both children needed to understand. It would not have taken long, once she had her facts collected, to say to the children (always, of course, getting down on their level and establishing good eye contact), "Have you been having fun while you are screaming and fighting each other?"

Even the angriest child will still realize that it's not good fun to hit and yell. So Mom could continue, "Dennis, I know you're two, and it's not easy to share when you're that little, but let me show you something!" With a smile, Mom could take the ball, sit on the floor, and establish a three-way path for rolling it back and forth among all three of them. In only a minute, she would be able to return to her work with the children playing happily (at least for a time).

That way everyone learns how to choose—Mom chooses to teach her children, not just to punish; the children choose to play together rather than fighting. And in ten years, those children will be more capable of making many wise choices.

How can you help? At all age levels, guide your children in careful, intelligent decision making. By asking thoughtful questions in an honest and friendly manner, you can teach your children that they can make even small decisions successfully with positive outcomes. As you master this technique, you'll even feel better about your job

as parent. And it'll save you the emotional and destructive
energy of screaming at your kids!

Emotions Affect Choice

Most decisions would be made more wisely if people waited
long enough to gain control of their emotions. Take this
situation as an example: Emily and Dan have been playing
far too roughly in the house. Dad has warned them several
times, but they don't obey him. Then a costly table lamp, a
prized wedding gift, is knocked to the floor! It's broken
beyond repair. Dad is furious! He tells the children, eight
and ten, that they are grounded to their rooms for a month.
Both children are angry and scared. They feel they were
only having fun and that Dad is so unfair. They didn't mean
to do it! (Secretly, they're already plotting ways to sneak
out or get around the restriction.)

In this situation, both the father and the children have
made choices. The children decided to ignore their dad's
warning; the father decided to get angry and blow up at the
kids. If Dad had sent Emily and Dan to their rooms, allowed
his anger to subside, and *then* decided what to do, the
situation may have gone more like this:

*Dad asks the children to sit near him while he explains.
"Dan and Emily, I like to see you play and hear you laugh,
but I feel very sad when you don't listen to me. Now our
lamp is broken. Your grandparents gave it to Mother and
me for our wedding, and we can never replace it. Now
suppose you two tell me what you can learn from this."*

By asking good questions and making suggestions like this,
the father could have enabled his children to arrive at some

excellent decisions regarding future play activities. Dad, too, could have learned to take firmer action *before* something happened—instead of issuing only a warning.

Whether the emotion experienced is anger, anxiety, fear, or excitement, it may impair wise decision making. At any age, on all occasions, wait for your feelings to calm down before choosing any plan of action. Your decisions will be all the better for it!

Learn from the Past

If you can remember similar situations from your past, you can choose far more successfully. It is the mistakes we make that seem to teach us the most unforgettable lessons. But you can learn from successes as well—both your own and others. And early on you can help your children to recognize similarities in events involving choices. Without even implying "I told you so!" you can help a child recall what happened when he failed to study for a test, or when she repeated gossip about a friend.

There are so many lessons to work out in life that it's a shame to repeat mistakes. This is especially true in the area of choices. Wrong choices can create disaster!

Good Role Models

A good role model is priceless! When children see parents choosing badly, they are more than likely to follow suit. If you, as a parent, choose to watch TV or take long naps when you need to do household tasks or spend time with your family, imagine what your children will choose.

A wise proverb says, "They sow the wind and reap a whirlwind" (Hosea 8:7a). So think ahead ten or fifteen years. If your child does as you do, only many times more intensely, what will his or her life be like? Your own choices will be much better if you answer that question honestly.

Before you take the easy way out of tough situations, before you decide to drink a little or indulge in too much medication to "calm your nerves," before you decide to be less than totally honest, before you engage in "harmless" flirtation, *think!* What will your negative choice teach your son or daughter? Your choosing to practice honesty, consideration, and love will enable your children to follow in your footsteps more easily.

Parental Indulgence

Giving in to a baby and pampering him or her is easy and very tempting. It's fun to see Baby Sarah smile and difficult to deny her the things she seems to want. Without realizing it, parents can begin building a weak foundation for choices. By indulging a child's every whim, he will learn to expect everyone to give in to his wishes and emotional storms. Such children become monsters at two and get out of control in the teens.

One truly great definition of maturity is this: *Maturity is the postponement of present pleasure for future good.* This philosophy contains the very heart of successful choosing. Can you teach your child to delay what she would like to do, in the interest of her best welfare? For example, your daughter wants to play with her friends; your son would rather talk on the phone. They'd both rather watch TV than study or rake leaves. What will you do? If you always permit them to choose present pleasure when they are young, children develop habits that are increasingly difficult to break.

You can build sturdy foundations of healthy character by training your children to assume proper degrees of responsibility as they grow. This building demands your time and hard work. If you, yourself, have not achieved mature stature, you will have difficulty making yourself do such a tough task. However, if you fail to do so, you may have great heartache later on (especially in the turbulent teen years). So we encourage you to find the courage and strength. Train up your children well!

Build Self-Control

Build self-control into your child. So many poor choices are the result of impulsiveness and a major lack of self-control. When wishes are strong and emotions are intense, the cool logic and disciplined will required for good decisions are hard to find. But you must teach these qualities to your children.

How do children learn self-control?

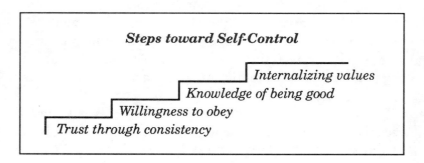

Steps toward Self-Control

Internalizing values
Knowledge of being good
Willingness to obey
Trust through consistency

First, the child must learn to trust through the parents' consistency and love. Then out of that trust grows the child's willingness to give up some of his will in order to obey Mom and Dad (or, simply, "to be good"). Out of this ability to be good just out of respect and love comes information. For example, your child realizes, "I feel good when I act good. Things go better around here. It's worth the effort." Out of that knowledge comes the process of "internalizing." Your child takes into his own self the values he learns from you and others.

This is the process by which children learn self-control. Of course, you as a parent must continue to watch and persevere so that this powerful quality will stay active in your child. Self-control is of ultimate importance, for it is out of healthy self-control that kindness, love, and compassion grow, facilitating decisions that are good for others, as well as one's self.

Avoid Manipulating

Children are smart—they have many distinct ways of getting what they want. Sometimes a child learns to get her way by being charming. Another child throws a tantrum. Both want their selfish ends, no matter how much that gain may hurt others. If you let your child get away with either end of the spectrum, you're encouraging a negative habit. Your children will learn to manipulate you—and others.

Learning to manipulate prevents clearcut wise decisions. Rather than focusing on *what is right* in a given situation, children learn to think in terms of *who will win*. Hence, power struggles develop that prevent any real winning. Without meaning to do so, many parents teach this habit to their children. They actually try to gain compliance from their children by threats or abuse, rather than firmly and clearly requiring right decisions and actions. Or they bribe their children by offering rewards, often of extreme value for small duties.

What about you? Do you allow your child to manipulate you and others in your home? Are you a manipulator?

Teaching Choices

Obedience, good behavior, and respect are all based on tiny good choices. A toddler chooses to put away toys and take a nap first because Mom requires it. As she grows older, she puts clothes away because she learns to like a neat environment.

Getting a child to do or behave rightly is directly related to teaching right choices. And teaching right choices demands these actions from you as a parent:

- *Words.* Teach your child what you expect and give a good reason. (This is the step of information about choosing.)

- *Examples.* When you practice what you preach to your child, he will learn more rapidly what he should do.

- *Action.* All children prefer their own way. If they would rather play than take a nap or finish a job, that is understandable. But do you want your child to make that choice? If so, he will learn to be irresponsible. You may physically have to take the child to bed and make him take a nap. Or you may have to stay with her until she completes the task.

- *Reward.* Giving up our own way and giving in to authority is no fun. We all like to resist authority. But we must all live with it. You can submit to an unfair boss because you know there will be a paycheck. But what about your child? Your child also needs a pay-check—and the very best one is your approval. So when your child has the most difficulty giving in, that may be the time he most needs you to express pride that, at last, he did so. Never mind for now that he did it less than graciously.

When you think clearly yourself, make good decisions, and consistently follow through, you can prevent many of the hindrances that will impair your child's choices.

Part II

The C~SOCC~ Approach

Choices are the Hinges of Destiny.
EDWIN MARKHAM

S = Situation—A Dangerous Opportunity

O = Options—A Gamut of Possibilities

C = Choice—Power over Destiny

C = Consequences—The Law of Life

C = Consistency—The Parental Commitment

– 5 –
Situation—
A Dangerous Opportunity

*H*omework—a word that is heard in every home and
school in the nation

Homework—a simple word, understood by parents and
children alike

Homework—a word that can engender procrastination,
lying, hostility, and rebellion in a five-year-old as well as
a fifteen-year-old

Homework—a word that can trigger frustration, anger,
screaming, and ultimatums in the parent of a young
child and in the parent of a teen

Perhaps you and your children have experienced one or
more of the seven harrowing homework hassles:

- You and your children engage in nightly battles over
when homework will be done.

- Your children rush through homework assignments, with sloppy, incomplete results.

- Your children "forget" to bring their homework assignments home.

- You do more of the homework than your children do.

- Your children take forever to finish their homework assignments.

- Your children insist that they are able to do homework while watching TV, talking on the phone, and listening to the stereo.

- The first time you hear about a major project is the night before it's due . . . and it isn't finished.[1]

No doubt many of you can already feel your frustration rising, just thinking about how you can MAKE your children study tonight. And getting kids to do homework is only *one* example of the situations that can occur on any given day in the life of a parent and child!

How can we, as parents, deal with troublesome issues?

Dangerous Opportunities

We should consider all troublesome issues as *dangerous opportunities*. Why? First let's look at what we mean by *dangerous*.

Troublesome issues are *dangerous* because we parents have the power to tear down our children's sense of self-worth, of belonging, of feeling loved. We also have the power to promote irresponsibility, to nurture destructive parental dependence, to protect our children from responsibility for their own actions. We can sow seeds of anger, hurt, hostility, and lack of trust and respect for authority.

Why are situations like the homework crisis *opportunities?* They provide an opportunity to build up your child's sense of self-worth, of belonging, of being loved. Parents have the opportunity to foster independence, responsibility, self-control, and to encourage trust and respect for authority.

It is no wonder that in Chinese calligraphy, the words *dangerous opportunity* are joined together to make the word *crisis!* As parents, we have a dangerous opportunity— a crisis—in which we can negatively tear down a child or build positively into his life.

Parenting Styles

Our response to the awesome parenting challenge that is inherent in each and every situation depends largely on our parenting style. Parenting styles vary all the way from the *autocratic* style at one extreme to the *permissive* style at the other.

An Autocratic Parent

- *Desires absolute control*
- *Must be all-powerful, all-knowing*
- *Discourages questioning*
- *Insists on dependence*
- *Frowns upon freedom of choice*

Autocratic parents desire absolute control of their child. They tell the child what to do, what to think, and how and when to do it and think it. They also strongly discourage the child from questioning their values or from giving a differing opinion. They frown upon freedom of choice. Independence of thought or action is not permitted; they insist that the child must depend on them. They must be the all-powerful and all-knowing figure in the life of their child.

This approach leads to frequent battles, especially as the child matures (and desires some independence and a part in the decision-making process). Power struggles become more and more common as time goes by. The parent is often heard to make such remarks as, "Do it or else!" Or, "Because I said so!" The older child will challenge with, "You can't make me!" And very, very often, "You don't understand!"

While autocratic parenting seems easier, more powerful, and even protective, it is not helpful in teaching choices. True, a rare child may learn what is best from the parent's decisions. But many more will undoubtedly lose sight of decision making by either giving up in despair or rebelling. Helping a child learn how to choose wisely is the real challenge of healthy parenting.

A Permissive Parent

- *Wants child to be happy above all else*
- *Lets child do his own thing*
- *Not concerned with order, routine*
- *Allows child to rule*
- *Is inconsistent*
- *Permits total freedom*

Permissive parents want their child "to be happy" above all else. They believe that letting the child "do his own thing" is the best child-rearing approach. They aren't consistent in requiring the child to share, to cooperate, or to respect authority. Basically, the child rules the household, which revolves entirely around her wishes and whims. Permissive parents are minimally concerned about order and establishing routines and allow the child the freedom to run wherever and whenever she pleases.

This parenting style is likely to produce a child who has an unwieldy sense of power. She knows how to get her way, but by doing so consistently, she senses that the adults in her world are weak. Young and inexperienced as she is, she is more powerful than her parents.

You might think that children would like this kind of power. Actually, feeling all this power is frightening and produces guilt. A child with permissive parents wishes that Mom and Dad would take a stand at least once in a while, even though she will test them to the limit!

This parenting style actually produces an insecure child who grows up with almost no sense of how she fits, without the skills necessary to be a successful part of a working, sharing, cooperating society. The child raised permissively becomes more and more hostile as time goes by when any demands are made of her. Her parent might respond in hurt frustration, "After all I've done for you" to the child's challenges of "I won't!", "Says who?", and "What are you going to do about it?"

The Parent/Child Standoff

In reality, parents may switch back and forth between autocratic parenting and permissive parenting. Such inconsistency depends on the amount of information they have, their mood, how much time is involved, what else is happening in their lives at the moment, their physical health, and how important they believe the situation is to the future of the child and to the comfort and well being of the family.

Many a parent comes home from work exhausted—just in time to hear complaints that classes are too hard, her daughter doesn't care for the teacher, and her son has to go out to a meeting after dinner. Because she's lacking in energy, a tired parent may be more tolerant about a child not doing his homework than the parent who feels reasonably well, believes in the importance of the homework, supports the teacher, will be home all evening, and has time to answer a homework question.

Mixed messages are sent to the child when one parent tends to be autocratic while the other is usually permissive. In such a home, the child soon learns to pit the permissive parent against the autocratic to get her own way. This early use of manipulation is detrimental for the child in developing healthy inter-personal relationships later in life. It creates guilt and resentments in both child and parent.

Since homework hassles are universal to all parents, let's use that as an example. The autocratic father may say, "Go to your room and do your homework." Seeing the permissive mother in the background, Steven begins to whine and whimper, "But I don't know how to do it, and I'm too tired and hungry!" The father doesn't stand for nonsense. "You heard what I said!" he barks. "Get to your room now, or you'll be sorry!" Steven begins to cry as he moves toward the bedroom.

The permissive mother is moved by the pleas of the child and attempts to follow him. The father speaks loudly and with great authority, "Leave Steven alone. The main reason he can't do anything for himself is that you won't stop babying him." The mother backs off, heads for the kitchen, prepares a plate for the poor child, and, as soon as possible, sneaks into the child's room, providing food and help with homework. What she doesn't realize is that all the while she is tearing down the father's authority and any semblance of family harmony. She is training the child that there is always a way around obedience.

Whether a parent behaves differently from time to time (switches between autocratic and permissive) or whether one parent is markedly easier or tougher than the other doesn't matter. The result is the same. Every child needs consistency. A child raised with inconsistency will feel anxious and will act out such anxiety either by acting aggressively or by withdrawing. Living at either extreme makes rational thinking and decision making difficult.

Whether the autocratic or permissive style of parenting is chosen, the child is thwarted from learning to become an independent, responsible individual, who is accountable for his or her choices, and is mature enough to accept the consequences of those decisions.

The Approach

You may be thinking, "Great! I can't win! So what am I supposed to do?" But there is another way. The SOCCC style of parenting provides a balance between the autocratic and permissive styles.

The **SOCC** *Parent*

- *Balances freedom and responsibility*
- *Teaches control and guides the child*
- *Accepts criticisms and suggestions*
- *Encourages thinking before acting*
- *Allows child to ask questions and form opinions*
- *Believes happiness is a by-product of self-esteem, confidence, assuming responsibility for choices, and being productive*
- *Insists that the family operate as a team*
- *Is consistent*
- *Refuses to rescue child from natural consequences*
- *Is cooperation, respect, trust*

The SOCCC parent believes in individual freedom and teaches it, but always in conjunction with the responsibility that the privilege of freedom brings, and always in regard for the rights of others. The child's freedom is always contained within limits. The SOCCC parent wants the child to learn ultimately to be in control in all situations of life.

SOCCC parents encourage their child to think about the situation before acting and to think through the consequences inherent in each action. They encourage the child to ask questions, to understand the "why"s of everything, and to form opinions based on sufficient information and parental input. They believe that a child needs a great deal of guidance in small, steady steps, before the child is capable of "doing his own thing."

SOCCC parents have good self-esteem and don't need to be all-powerful and all-knowing. They are able to accept suggestions from a child and are even able to accept appropriate criticism and say, "We're sorry!" They value consistency and always strive to say what they mean and mean what they say. They are good role models of cooperation, respect, and trust. They insist that the family operate as a team, with each member contributing according to his ability to meet the needs of the others and achieve the goals of the family.

Overall, SOCCC parents believe that happiness is not a *goal*, but a *by-product* of self-esteem. This confidence results from making wise choices and from assuming responsibility for the consequences of all choices—good or bad.

Comparing Parenting Styles

The three parenting styles may be visualized in the following way:

Parenting Styles

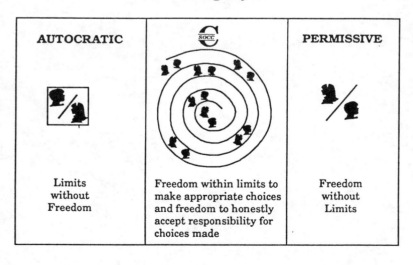

AUTOCRATIC	SOCCC	PERMISSIVE
Limits without Freedom	Freedom within limits to make appropriate choices and freedom to honestly accept responsibility for choices made	Freedom without Limits

Let's go back to the homework situation and see how these three distinct parenting styles would be applied.

The *autocratic* parent would apply insistent, incessant pressure on the child to get the work done. This pressure could be applied in a variety of ways.

The *permissive* parent might think the assignment really isn't very important. Since the child is tired and doesn't want to do it, why bother?

The *SOCCC* parent looks at the homework assignment as one way to encourage responsibility, dependability, and self-control in the child.

Which type of parent would you rather be? As an autocratic parent, you may become frazzled because *you* are always the one putting pressure on the kids. As a permissive parent, your child will tromp all over you—and others someday. As a SOCCC parent, you will have more control and freedom. We'll talk more about this approach in the rest of this book.

S = Situation—A Dangerous Opportunity
O = Options—A Gamut of Possibilities
C = Choice—Power over Destiny
C = Consequences—The Law of Life
C = Consistency—The Parental Commitment

– 6 –
Options—
A Gamut of Possibilities

Should I get a job after school or try out for basketball?
Everybody's doing it, but should I be like everyone else?
Should I play with Tommy or Susie today?
Should I buy this toy or save up for something big?
Should I do my homework myself (even though I'm bad at math) or just copy from Janie (who's a math whiz?)
Should we take an inexpensive family vacation this year— or save up to go to Hawaii in two years?

"What are my options?" is a familiar question and an exceedingly important one. A certain variety of options are inherent in every situation. Whether they are parental options, your child's options, or options for the whole family, there are a gamut of possibilities.

Past Choices Affect Present Options

But those options are not totally free. They are loaded down with past habits that greatly affect the present available options. For example, not doing homework would never be an option for a conscientious student. But an unmotivated student who lacks parental support and direction would not even consider doing "boring" homework. He wouldn't think of it as an option.

Prior choices also limit the number of options. As the child gets older, there will be more options or fewer options depending on the wisdom exercised in previous choices. A student who will not get up in front of the class will not have the option of winning the school speech contest. A student who does not participate in the sports program will not be concerned with try-outs, games, and interscholastic competitions. Good choices broaden the scope of options and opportunities. Poor choices limit the options and restrict the opportunities.

Marla and Tom, for example, both wanted to earn spending money while in high school. So they applied for work in the same fast-food restaurant and were accepted. Marla was disappointed with the "boring" work she was expected to do. She constantly complained and showed disinterest while working. Tom realized he was on the bottom rung of the restaurant ladder, was not offended by the work, and did it to the best of his ability.

The result? In a short time, Marla's hours were cut back, while Tom's were extended. Marla was disgusted by the "unfair treatment" and quit. While she hopped from job to job, continuing to receive entry-level wages and positions, Tom stayed with the fast-food restaurant, receiving wage increases and more responsibility.

By the time Tom was ready to go away for college, his experience enabled him to assume a responsible position in a hotel restaurant. Marla was still flitting from job to job, never satisfied, always complaining, and never staying long enough to benefit from wage increases or responsibility advancement.

Peer Pressure

The strong influence of your child's peer group as he moves into adolescence will also greatly affect his options. If the peer group places a high value on education and grades, the child will strive to conform (or else will move out of the pressure of that peer group into one that doesn't stress learning as much). Likewise, if the child's peer group ridicules academic efforts, the child will be far less motivated to excel unless he switches peer groups.

Limitations

Physical, mental, emotional, and financial resources place further limitations on the options available. Maybe your child has been born with a physically weak constitution that makes him tire more easily than the other kids. If your child is physically handicapped, her participation in sports will be somewhat restricted. Your son's learning disability in high school may cause you to rethink any involvement in special academic programs (or hopes for scholarships). Emotional difficulties also affect all areas of life. Many parents would like to offer their children special opportunities but can't because of financial limitations.

Your Child's Options

At any given time, your child has a wide variety of options.
Let's discuss just a few of them.

Sports or other extra-curricular activities. To join the
team or not to join the team, that is one question. Enrolling
a child in scouts, music lessons, gymnastics, or dancing
classes are other options. If you see a specific talent for one
of these areas in your child, you have an important option
to examine. We recommend that you help your children
explore a variety of interests and abilities. When a focus
becomes clear, encourage your child to concentrate on the
development of that skill. Following up on options demands
some parental authority as well as the child's choosing.
Most children love to explore new opportunities but they
rarely pursue them to the point of excellence without a lot
of encouragement.

If you plan to keep a rich range of options open to your
child, you need to establish some policies regarding practice, standards of excellence, and tenacity. Parents who
follow through with such basic guidance will not only teach
their children to develop healthy self-esteem now but will
also enlarge their future possibilities!

Social skills. There is a climate of immense freedom
today to choose wrong over right, and this is complicated
by poor teaching regarding values. Just what makes something *right* or *wrong?* If "everyone is doing it," does that
mean it's okay? Parents, you need to give your children
basic teaching about right and wrong early on (or as soon
as you can begin). Being either autocratic or permissive will
not work! You must give your family tools for reasoning out
the answers.

Any option is a negative one if it is damaging or if it lessens the potential for future good. If a child fails to choose wisely among the many options available, he or she will certainly mar the future. If a young person chooses the option of smoking, chemical use, or sexual promiscuity, her future is likely to become seriously impaired.

Pretending to be a friend, while gossiping behind that friend's back, is a poor choice. Wanting to be popular is a dangerous temptation (even though it's natural). If reaching that goal results in falseness and superficiality, it's not a positive option. Spending money beyond one's resources in order to acquire name-brand clothing (because everybody else has it) is another example of an available option that wouldn't be wise.

How will you teach your child about such options? First you must see them clearly yourself. Your lifestyle will teach a set of options to your children. Step back and observe your own values. How do you decide on priorities regarding time and money expenditures? How often do you discuss values with your family? What do you talk about during dinner? Options can be clarified by family discussions of values and priorities.

Family harmony. In today's Western world, family life has been dealt mortal blows. Divorce, liberal values, materialism, and self-centered philosophies have destroyed close to one family out of two. You as parents also have options. You can carry on business affairs or a social life that risks your marriage and destroys the positive role model your children need. You can choose to live selfishly, no matter what the price. Or you can face the option of commitment to your family that lays the foundation for their future options. The best options are rarely easy!

Lifestyle Options

What are the options available in any family's lifestyle?

- Each can pursue his or her own affairs, rarely interacting with other family members and experiencing little, if any, intimacy.

- Family members can engage in frequent power struggles, each seeking his own way. Usually this lifestyle involves varying degrees of manipulation or "bullying" and always results in hurts and estrangement.

- There can be superficial "niceness" while people walk on proverbial egg shells to avoid any hurt feelings but sacrifice the level of honesty that is so vital to family health.

- The healthiest family cares about each individual's welfare as well as the strength of the family as a whole. Family members are willing to confront and disagree, but they stick with the issues and with each other until agreement is reached and harmony restored.

As you and your children make choices from all available options, each choice paves the way for increasing opportunities, or for decreasing opportunities in quality and quantity. Guiding children to make wise choices is the heart of the SOCCC approach.

S = Situation—A Dangerous Opportunity

O = Options—A Gamut of Possibilities

C = Choice—Power over Destiny

C = Consequences—The Law of Life

C = Consistency—The Parental Commitment

– 7 –
Choice—
Power over Destiny

Decisions determine destiny.
FREDERICK SPEAKMAN

All of life is a series of choices. From the first moment of consciousness at the beginning of day until we are lulled into sleep in late evening, we are besieged with a variety of choices.

Some of these choices can be fun to make:

"Shall I travel here or there?"
"Shall I order à la carte?"
"Shall I buy this or that?"

Other choices are mundane:

"Which shall I do first—the dishes or the laundry?"
"Should I call the plumber before I arrange for the car to be repaired?"
"Which tasks will I complete today?"

Some choices are challenging:

*"What are my choices for motivating my children to
   do their chores?"*
"Will I do what's necessary to get better employment?"

Still other choices are painful:

"Shall I pay this bill or that one?"
"Am I ready to kick the habit?"
"Will I give up this person?"

All Choices Are Interdependent

No matter what type of choice it is, every choice we make
is important. Why? Because our lives *today* are the very
result of the choices of all our *yesterdays,* and our *tomor-
rows* will be the result of the choices we make *today.*

The same is true for our children. Making choices for
ourselves and our children is serious business. If you have
been making poor choices, don't despair. Today can be the
first day of your new life as a SOCCC parent! So begin now
to make smart choices because choices are not child's play.

Choices have far greater implications than the effects
they have on our own lives. Our choices also shape the lives
of the people who share our world. Those deeply affected
by our choices include our children, spouses (current and/or
ex), family, friends, employers, and employees.

As this story illustrates, no choice exists in a vacuum.

Sheri's mother was downright disgusted. Her twelve-
year-old daughter was the queen of procrastination. Sheri
always waited until the last possible moment to do every-

thing, which usually meant racing through chores or slopping through homework on the ride to school.

This had to stop! Sheri's mother, motivated by months of frustrating failures, announced to her daughter one morning, "You are not—I repeat *not*—leaving this house until your room is cleaned!" The daughter was aghast. "What about the car pool?" Her mother countered, "They will just have to wait or leave, so you'd better get working!" Steaming and sputtering, Sheri frantically began the work, accompanied by her mother's repeated tirade about how she'd told her a thousand times, etc., etc.

The car pool arrived. Of course, Sheri wasn't ready. The driver and two other girls waited a few minutes, then one girl came to the door to find out what was happening. The mother recounted the story, satisfied that she had arrived at a solution that would solve her daughter's problem of procrastination.

But not everything went as planned. The car pool waited until a crying Sheri stormed out of the house screaming, "I hate my mother! It's her fault if we're late to school! She never told me until *this* morning I had to clean my room before I left!"

The car pool finally did arrive at school. But three girls were late to class—and the driver was late to work.

Sheri's choice to procrastinate was wrong—and it affected her mother. Because Sheri's mom was frustrated with the situation, she made an impetuous choice. The result? Rather than learning to establish an efficient work and play schedule, her daughter was humiliated and angered. And innocent car-pool participants were also affected. They chose to wait, and all were late.

Some people choose procrastination in an attempt to postpone the unpleasantness of a situation. Sheri's procrastination, however, resulted in more pain for her and others than if she had just done the work earlier.

Sheri's mom, too, had other options. She could have given Sheri the ultimatum the evening before, or after school. She might have driven Sheri to school herself late that morning (after Sheri had finished her task). The mother's choice to make others late was both inconsiderate and embarrassing (especially to the daughter). Both Sheri and her mother discovered options that did *not* work; hopefully they will investigate some different options the next time a tense situation arises between them.

Not Making a Choice Is Making a Choice

Occasionally a parent or child will attempt to avoid making a choice. "Let's not talk about it," or "I don't want even want to think about it," are comments heard when pressure is being exerted to make a decision. What they're really hoping is, "If I don't think about it, 'it' will go away!" No way! Failure to make a choice *is* a choice. It is a choice to abdicate responsibility, allowing the relentless drift of events to shape our lives, rather than assuming the control and responsibility ourselves.

Persistent abdication of responsibility can develop into a habit that leads to a crippling inability to make decisions. That's what happened to Steven.

Steven was an adorable baby, growing up in a loving home. When Steven was a toddler, he began to reach out and grab for things. His well-meaning parents didn't want to thwart his development and didn't understand the importance of providing choices and of teaching Steven to make choices, so they used the technique of distraction.

When Steven reached for a breakable object, they would say, "Look over here, Steven. You like trucks; let's play with the big truck." This worked for a time. Unfortunately, the distraction technique becomes less and less effective the more it was used, and all too soon it became useless with Steven. He knew what he wanted to touch and see and would not be distracted.

Since passive control was not working, Steven's parents began to be assertive. Still, Steven was given no choices. His parents didn't know how they could give him choices and yet remain in control. Now his parents would say, "Don't touch that, Steven . . . Steven, get your hands off of that . . . Steven, I'm counting . . . 1, 2, 3 . . . Steven, I'm counting, and when I get to 10 you're getting slapped . . . $8\frac{1}{2}$, $8\frac{3}{4}$, 9 . . . Steven, I mean it. Get your hands off!" By the time they got to "9 and $\frac{7}{8}$," Steven had lost interest in whatever he was touching and was ready to move on to the next object.

The parents realized their "discipline" wasn't working, but they didn't know what to do. "I guess he's just a strong-willed child," they would say to friends whose children were obedient. By the time Steven was five years old, the screams and threats had accelerated, but Steven's behavior had not improved. If anything, he was more in charge of the household than ever.

Steven's rebellion toward his parents was increasing. His parents were becoming more frustrated and helpless, wondering what had happened and what they could do. "I don't know what to do with him," his mother blurted out to a friend. With that comment, Steven's mother made the first large step on the road toward abdicating responsibility for her son and his choices, and showed her friends she could not make decisions.

But poor Steven! He received the raw end of this deal—he had never been given a choice. He'd been given distractions and warnings, and countings, and slaps—but no choices. If such a pattern continues in a home, a child's rebellion will grow. The parent/child standoff is a direct result of the power struggle that occurs in a home where the child grows up with no choices and, consequently, with no responsibility for his own behavior.

But what *could* the parents have done? What choice can a toddler be given? Doesn't a toddler need to touch and handle and explore?

A toddler is plenty smart. Certainly Steven was acting smarter than his parents, and he was obviously able to manipulate them to get his own way. Everywhere a toddler goes, there are things to touch, many of which are breakable, and too delicate for a two-year-old to handle. The parent needs to prepare the child ahead of time for what he will see and for the desired behavior. For example, the parent could say:

We are going to the store. You are going to see many things. You are going to see trucks. You may touch the trucks. You may not touch the other things. You may look at them with your eyes, but not your hands. If you touch the other things, then you will not be able to touch and play with the trucks becuase we will leave the store right away. If you do not touch the other things, then you may touch the trucks and play with them.

Now that's giving a child a choice. It gives him control over his destiny in the store. If he touches the other things, playing with the trucks is out. If he chooses to keep his hands off of the other things, then he can play with the trucks. And most children would choose to play with the trucks, and keep their hands off the other things!

Flexing Your Choice Muscles

Choice giving and choice making are like muscles. Both must be exercised in order to function well. The principle is simple: "Use it or lose it!" If the parent exercises choice-giving power, it grows and strengthens. If the choice-making muscle is exercised, it grows and strengthens; otherwise it will never develop, but will be replaced with rebellion and the inability to make wise decisions.

Making choices within boundaries can begin with a toddler. With choice, two-year-old Steven could have had power over his destiny in a positive way that encouraged obedience and discouraged rebellion. With choice giving, the parent encourages the child to accept responsibility, not abdicate it, and the parent accepts the responsibility for raising a child who makes wise decisions.

Let's compare the response of an autocratic mother, a permissive mother, and a SOCCC parent in an identical parenting situation.

The chill of autumn is in the air. Mothers across the nation silently unite to provide their little ones with a "good, hot breakfast," e.g., oatmeal or some similar concoction. A majority of preschoolers also unite in vocal opposition to this idea.

In the autocratic home, the conscientious mother has verified the weather report, checked outside to confirm it, and has the cereal ready. She proudly announces, "It's cold out today, so you'll have a nice hot breakfast." Three-year-old Jeffrey takes one look at the goo-like mixture and gives his verdict: "I hate this yucky stuff." Mom doesn't want an

early morning confrontation that wastes a lot of time, so
she tries a reasonable approach. "All the big boys eat hot
cereal, and you will too." At this point, Jeffrey doesn't care
what the so-called "big boys" are eating and wants no part
of the porridge. He says defiantly, "I *won't* eat this yucky
stuff." Mom becomes adamant: "You *will* eat it, and you will
eat it *right now!*" And there goes the power struggle—off
to an early morning start.

In the permissive home, Mom is already running late.
Since oatmeal is easy and available, it's hastily assembled.
She coaxes her disheveled son to the table saying, "Mommy
has made something really special for you today." Three-
year-old Jason is not impressed. (He's already heard that
story at least a million times). He looks disinterestedly in
the bowl and revolts. "I don't want any of that stuff!" Mom
moves instantly into her cajoling method of operation.
"Your friend Ryan eats it." Jason responds, "I don't care. I
won't eat it!" Mom takes a taste. "Mmm-good. Try just one
bite for Mommy."

Jason adamantly shakes his head, mouth closed. "It will
make you a big boy like Daddy. Do it for Daddy." No way.
After a few more futile attempts, Mom unloads her last
option. "Mommy will buy you something at the toy store if
you eat three bites." At this point, depending if there is
something he really wants at the toy store, Jason may eat
a bite or two (not three), grimacing the entire time, while
Mom tells him how "wonderful" he is!

The mother in the SOCCC home knows the weather
forecast but, more importantly, she knows her son, Brock.
She also knows that almost no human being on earth likes
being told exactly what to do, where to go, or what to eat.
She knows that Brock responds to choices and likes to feel
the "big boy" control of making decisions. She also knows

it's important to give him very simple decisions at his tender age of three. Yes, she would like to have him eat oatmeal or something similar, but she knows that the vitamin content of other cereals she purchases is similar, so it becomes more a matter of taste than a nutritional problem.

So what does this SOCCC mom do? She gives Brock a choice of two cereals, one that she knows he likes and one that she would like him to cultivate a taste for, e.g., oatmeal. She says, "This morning we're having cereal. Would you like Corn Whammies or oatmeal?" The chances are very likely that Brock will select what he already likes. So what? We all like to eat what we like, and not everyone enjoys trying new things, especially in the morning. Why would a three-year-old be any different? Brock has been given a choice, based on equal nutritional value. He has chosen, has felt the independence and power in making a decision, will eat the cereal, and be on his way. A power struggle has been avoided.

Parental Styles Regarding Choices

The three parental styles—autocratic, permissive, and SOCCC—vary widely in the way they teach children about choices.

The autocratic parent doesn't believe in choice giving, but only in choice making, and the choice made is always the same. "I want you to do it, and do it now, and do it my way—or else!" There is no place for choice giving since the child is often told "there will be no discussion! No ifs, ands, or buts!"

The permissive parent doesn't believe in choice making or choice giving either. He or she wants to abdicate responsibility and "just wait and see what happens." You'll hear a permissive parent say, "I'll be glad when he's through this stage!" What the permissive parent fails to understand is that if the problems of "this stage" and age are not resolved, those same problems will continue and intensify in the next stage of development. If a two-year-old is allowed to continue in rebellion, he will become a defiant teenager with no respect for any authority.

In the SOCCC approach the parent gives the child limited, age-appropriate choices, and allows the child to make his or her own decisions from the choices provided. It is crucial for parents to provide choices. Without gradually developing the skill to make good choices, children grow up making decisions based only on getting immediate pleasure and avoiding pain. The obvious fallacy of this pleasure vs. pain approach to decision making is that future pain is ignored entirely or grossly underestimated. For example, the immediate pleasure that comes from choosing not to do a homework assignment may be tinged with some amount of guilt, and is certain to become embarrassment the following day at school.

Your Child's Development

When a child grows up being allowed to make choices, essential areas of development are being strengthened many times during the day. What are these areas of development?

The child is respected. You show your child respect by allowing him to make decisions. Each time you give your child a choice, you are saying, "I believe in you as a person. I respect you enough to allow you to make a choice, and I believe that you will make a good decision."

The child's self-esteem grows. Success breeds success. With each choice given and made, the child feels loved and worthwhile—and this is the essence of self-esteem. Each good decision (whether to eat a certain cereal, to accomplish a task around the house, or to get and keep employment) builds self-esteem and gives the child greater confidence in his abilities to choose and to perform. Research from many sources has shown that children who perceive themselves as important, contributing parts of ongoing relationships before the age of twelve are more resistant to peer groups, cults, and extraneous programming during their teenage years than children who perceive themselves as insignificant.[1]

The child is motivated. Nothing decreases motivation like waking up in the morning knowing that you will be told what to do every moment with no part in the decision process.

Nothing increases motivation like knowing that you are the key factor in the decision process, and that those decisions will determine not only what you eat and wear, but what will happen to you during the day. The child who is responsible for consequences will also be motivated to make increasingly wiser decisions.

The power struggle is minimized. If the child is allowed to make choices, both parent and child are respected, have self-esteem, and are motivated. Just as an atmosphere of no choices is the breeding ground for rebellion, so the atmosphere of appropriate choices provides fertile soil for cooperation. Put yourself in the place of your child. Would you rather be given a choice of this or that, or be told that you would have to do this, do it this way, do it right now, and do it my way? Allowing a child to make choices, regardless of how seemingly insignificant, develops respect, self-esteem, and motivation. Providing appropriate choices can eliminate the parent/child standoff.

A Good Gift

Of all the gifts that a parent can give a child, the gift of learning to make good choices is the most valuable and long-lasting. Choice is a gift that a child will open each time a decision is needed. Choice is a gift that grows stronger with use, and it is up to the parent just how strong the gift will ultimately be. The way the gift of choice is given is exceedingly important. It must be given with wisdom and discretion on the part of the parent because, to a large degree, it will determine the destiny of the child, whether for good or for ill.

> *Of all the gifts that a parent can give a child, the gift of learning to make good choices is the most valuable and long-lasting.*

The gift of choice is not only a gift you give your child, but also a gift that affects others (as we discussed earlier). Each time your child makes a decision and assumes the responsibility for that choice, his character grows, and that small chip of character, building through the years of choice making, builds character and strength in society as a whole.

> *Choice is a gift that comes back to the parent as pride in a job well done. Not giving it will result in the piercing pain of disappointment.*

Steps toward Making Choices

At first the gift of choice is a small package for a very young child. The gift takes the form of "either . . . or." The choice given to the preschooler in the "cereal story" is typical of choices for young children:

- We will go *either* to this restaurant *or* that restaurant.

- We will have *either* hamburgers *or* hot dogs. Which do you want?

- Would you rather put away your clothes first *or* your toys first?

- You must finish *either* your vegetables *or* your meat before leaving the table.

- You must *either* help wash the dishes *or* dry the dishes. Which would you rather do?

You will notice that in the "either . . . or" choice, there is really no consequence. The choice not chosen is simply eliminated. The young child needs to build a foundation of making decisions, just as the new parent, or a parent new to the SOCCC approach, needs to learn how to give limited, appropriate choices. In the choices mentioned, there is no bad choice, merely two acceptable ones. That is the way it must begin for the mutual success of the parent and the child.

After both the parent and child have mastered the "either . . . or" choice making, both may move into the more complicated "when . . . then" form of choice making:

- *When* you have finished your breakfast, *then* you may go outside and play.

- *When* you have finished picking up your room, *then* I will help you clean it.

- *When* you have finished your homework, *then* you may turn on the TV.

- *When* you say, "Please," *then* you may leave the table.

- *When* you have completed all your chores, *then* you may take the car.

- *When* you can pay for the insurance, gas, and car repairs, *then* you may have a car.

- *When* you bring up your grades to "C"s (or whatever is realistic), *then* you may go here or there.

When offering a "when you have . . . then you may . . . " choice, always mention the less desirable activity before the more desirable.

With this more sophisticated "when . . . then" type of choice, a consequence is implied. It becomes obvious that until breakfast is finished, there will be no playing outside. The choice of whether this means five minutes or two hours is entirely up to the child because you as the parent have said, "When you have finished your breakfast, then you may go outside and play."

With the gift of choice, the parent does not "make 'em" do anything. The child chooses to do it. The gift of choice takes away rebellion and diffuses the power struggle.

Years ago, there was a boy named Larry who attended school in a one-room rural school house. The school marm expected instant obedience. If she didn't get it, she applied the ruler of correction to knuckles.

This "obstinate young feller" had been given many hits by the ruler, and still Larry did not obey as was expected. The teacher warned him that if he kept being defiant, he would be spanked in front of the entire school.

On one particular day, Larry kept getting out of his seat. The teacher warned him repeatedly, and still he defied. She did as she had said, spanking him hard and long in front of all the students, most of them younger. The school teacher then said in a stern voice, "I trust that you have learned your lesson. Now go back to your seat, and sit down for the rest of the day."

Larry went back to his seat with an angry look on his face, sat down, and yelled back at her, "I'm sitting down on the outside, but I'm standing up on the inside!"

Too many children today are "sitting down on the outside, but standing up on the inside" because they have not been given the gift of choice through the years, and they are rebelling. The authority figures in their lives have not allowed them freedom to make choices that show respect, build their self-esteem, motivate them, and minimize the power struggle.

They have not learned to make the small "either . . . or" choices. They have not experienced the implied consequences of the "when you have . . . then you may" form of choice making. They have never learned to make appropriate choices, so when they rebel, their choices bring disaster to their own lives, the lives of their parents, and to other lives they touch.

The Art of Choosing

Here are some guidelines to help you teach the art of choosing:

Collect the necessary information. Form a clear picture of the precise situation that exists—for example, your daughter's room is a mess, your son blasts your eardrums with his loud stereo, your family has a habit of fighting and yelling, you know you need a budget, or your son's social habits need to be changed. Whatever the situation, you need to define it clearly.

List the possible options. Make a detailed list of both good and poor possibilities from which the final choice will be made. Seeing poor options in writing frequently makes it easier to eliminate them.

Make the final choice. Eliminate all the poor options to make the ultimate choice easier. Smart choices depend on solid facts about the situation and the options, and you can make them better if you can anticipate the possible consequences. Some choices are reversible while others must be final. So it's wise to take plenty of time to make the important, life-forming choices.

Grace's father was a man of great wisdom. His words have often helped her: "God is never in a hurry and he doesn't expect us to rush either. Chances are, if you feel you have to decide something quickly, it's not God's will. He will give you all the time you need."

Live with the consequences. Poor decisions that become a habit are often the result of failure to face the results. Loving parents often misguidedly rescue children from the painful outcomes of bad choices. The natural consequences of decisions will teach you to reinforce the success of wise choices or avoid the pain of poor ones. Be careful, then, to give your child well-deserved praise for making difficult decisions, and never rescue your child from the consequences of foolish ones. Avoid saying, "I told you so!" Simply help your child to focus clearly on why and how the choice was made and to see accurately whether that choice worked. If it didn't work, help your child decide how to do it differently next time.

Review the entire process. Briefly review the choice your child has made. It's a great way to help him analyze past choices that will enhance future decision making. Avoid lectures and condemning attitudes. Gently and clearly help your child to realize what was good or poor in his decision-making skills.

At all but the most simplistic level, choosing involves consequences. We as parents can't escape the consequences of our choices. And neither can our children escape theirs. Permitting your child to assume the responsibility for the consequences of each choice he makes is the heart of the SOCCC approach to child rearing (and requires plenty of brains on the part of the parent!). We'll talk more about that in the next chapter.

S = Situation—A Dangerous Opportunity

O = Options—A Gamut of Possibilities

C = Choice—Power over Destiny

C = Consequences=The Law of Life

C = Consistency—The Parental Commitment

– 8 –

Consequences—
The Law of Life

We reap what we sow, more than we sow, later than we sow.
CHARLES STANLEY

The fundamental law of physics is also the Law of Life: "For every action, there is an opposite and equal reaction." Every choice results in at least one consequence, and, almost always, the consequences are multiple.

This Law of Life operates faithfully in nature as the Law of the Land. We cannot change it, nor do we try. We acknowledge its existence and power, and we operate believing it is true. Let's take sowing and reaping for example. When a gardener plants squash, he harvests squash, not potatoes or apples. A farmer sows wheat and reaps wheat, not rice or barley. The law is so obvious that we don't even think about it.

In physics, there is the universal law of gravity. We know it, and we respect it. A person who walks off a tall building is not going to change the law of physics, no no matter what he believes about gravity. And if he challenges that law, he'll experience severe consequences.

Sowing and Reaping

What seems so simple in nature and in physics is more complex in human behavior, yet just as true. The Law of Life operates just as faithfully as the Law of Gravity or the Law of the Land. "Sow a thought, reap an action. Sow an action, reap a habit. Sow a habit, reap a lifestyle. Sow a lifestyle, reap a destiny." A harvest of consequences comes from the grains of our choices and from the choices of our children.

A choice today is like a rock tossed in the pond of tomorrow. Its consequences will ripple through future days, months, years, and decades. The best way to avoid the anguish of unwise choices is to ask, Do I want to experience the consequences this choice will bring?

Some time ago, the media reported the story of a professional football player who was suspended for life because of habitual cocaine use. He had been warned repeatedly to no avail and had brought on himself the untimely end of an impressive and lucrative career. He told reporters, "It is sad that I did not take into account the consequences of taking drugs. I did not think about the health problems that would come, the loss of my physical capabilities, the loss of my career, the hardship on my family, and the suffering of my spouse. I just didn't think about any of the consequences. I just did it because it felt good for the moment."

> *Do you want to experience the consequences this choice will bring?*

This tragic story is repeated too many times in the lives of people today. They just don't think about the consequences. They choose to do something that sounds like fun, will provide adventure and excitement, is not hard, and is readily available. Afterward they are surprised at the avalanche of consequences.

We don't want our children to suffer the regret and sorrow of the consequences of poor choices. But we must take action—we must teach them to make wise choices from their earliest years and to assume the responsibility for the consequences of each choice. By making wise decisions, they can save themselves much unnecessary pain.

The Reward of Smart Choices

Smart choices both reward and protect. For example, the student who chooses to do homework is rewarded with better grades than the student who chooses to ignore the homework. One research study reveals that when low-ability students do just one to three hours of homework a week, their grades are usually as high as those of average-ability students who don't do homework. Similarly, when average-ability students do three to five hours of homework a week, their grades usually equal those of high ability students who don't do any homework. The following graph

shows that the students who choose to spend more time
studying at home achieve better national test results.

**Test Scores of 1982 Seniors in Reading, Science, and
Mathematics by Amount of Homework per Week**[1]

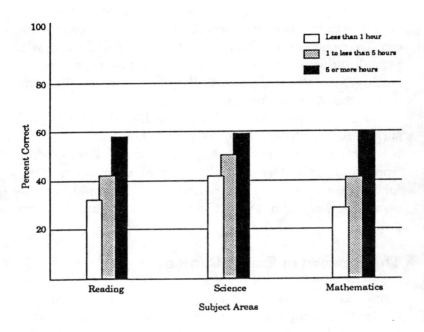

SOURCE: *Condition of Education, 1985* (U.S. Department of Education, National Center for
Education Statistics).

Persistence and determination have rewarding consequences. Just take a look at the encouraging results in the
lives of these famous people:

• When the great Polish pianist, Ignace Paderewski,
  first chose to study the piano, his music teacher told

him his hands were much too small to master the keyboard.

• When the great Italian tenor, Enrico Caruso, first applied for instruction, the teacher told him his voice sounded like the wind whistling through the window.

• When the great statesman of Victorian England, Benjamin Disraeli, attempted to speak in Parliament for the first time, members hissed him into silence and laughed when he said, "Though I sit down now, the time will come when you will hear of me." [2]

For the vast majority of us however, consequences of smart decisions are far less dramatic, though still as rewarding and satisfying. For example, Candice had no athletic inclination in elementary or junior high. But in high school, the cross-country coaches saw her run and encouraged her to join the team.

Cross-country running is a grueling sport that demands extraordinary endurance. Although Candice worked and worked the first year and improved her time, she always came in close to last. The following year she redoubled her effort and received the "Most Improved Player" award. The third year she ran many miles and participated in event after event but continued to be an average runner. The last year she improved even more, but she was still only an alternate in the finals.

What did Candice gain from all this? She learned to keep on in spite of difficulties, even though she knew she would never be first. She became close friends with the other runners. Finally, at the awards ceremony, she was honored with the high achievement of "Most Inspirational Player."

Wise decisions can protect your children physically, emotionally, mentally, and financially. The young person who has the courage to say, "No!" to drugs will be protected from the drug-induced deterioration of body, mind, and emotions, and is much less likely to be involved in the drug-related activities of theft and prostitution. The young person who has the self-esteem to say "No!" to premarital sex will be protected from the lifelong effects of guilt.

Anticipating Possible Outcomes of Choices

It's easy to forget one aspect of consequences—anticipating possible outcomes. Most of us don't want to take the time to anticipate what might happen if we make the wrong choice.

I (Grace) once worked in a home for young, unwed mothers. Many of these mothers had never dreamed they would become pregnant, much less mothers at such a young age. Most of them were ill-prepared to deal with such a responsibility. An intensely emotional aspect of their situation was that of choosing what to plan for their babies' future. Each expectant mother had to decide whether to relinquish her baby for adoption or try to keep and care for the baby on her own (most unwed mothers who keep their babies end up as single parents).

It was extremely important to encourage wise decisions in such a crucial choice that would profoundly impact not only her life, but that of her baby. So the counselors helped each young woman start two lists. One was focused on possible positive consequences if she kept her child. The other tallied negative aspects that could be expected. For many days, each mother worked on her lists. Although the lists didn't make the decisions easier, they made mature, wise decisions more possible.

Two Types of Consequences

Natural consequences and logical consequences are two categories you can use to guide your children toward making wise decisions.

Natural consequences. A *natural* consequence happens as a result of natural causes, usually from something in the environment. Your child can learn responsibility from natural consequences without your intervention.

Here are some examples of *natural* consequences:

- It's raining. Your child leaves the house without boots or umbrella. Getting wet is the natural consequence.

- The pot on the stove is hot. Your child touches the pot. Suffering the pain of a burn is the natural consequence.

- It's a very cold day. Your child forgets to take a coat. Getting cold is the natural consequence.

- Your child leaves the house without breakfast. Becoming hungry at school is the natural consequence.

- Your child leaves a wallet containing money on the school playground. Losing the money (and the wallet) is a natural consequence.

Well-meaning parents frequently don't allow their children to experience natural consequences. Out of hearts full of love and service to their children, these parents rescue their children from the necessary lessons of responsibility they can learn from experiencing consequences. Parents who rush in to save their children are really saying, "You can't take care of yourself. I can. See—you need me to help you!"

Repeatedly jumping in to rescue children from consequences enables them to remain dependent, vulnerable, and crippled in their development.

Logical consequences. Over 2000 years ago, one author said, "A man reaps what he sows" (Gal. 6:7). *Logical* consequences are related directly to the choice. For example, a person chooses to be friendly and outgoing. What is the consequence? That person will reap a harvest of friends. A person who chooses to be aloof and standoffish will reap a harvest of loneliness and restricted friendships.

Natural Consequences

Many of life's lessons can be taught most effectively if we let our children experience *natural* consequences without interference.

Once a science teacher sent his student into the woods to observe a cocoon. The student watched intently as the butterfly's wings began to break through the silken fibers. He watched and waited, then grew impatient. It was taking so long, and the butterfly was putting forth enormous effort with uncertain results. Unable to stand the seeming futility of the struggle any longer, the student reached in with a delicate finger and tenderly helped the butterfly out of the cocoon. Pleased with the result, he watched as the butterfly flew a few feet, then spiraled to the earth and died.

The student was aghast. What had happened? He hurried back to his teacher who explained, "When you reached in to help, you deprived the butterfly of the opportunity to strengthen its wings in the struggle that was essential for life."

Just as the butterfly had to struggle to gain strength for survival in the outside world, so our children must learn the difficult lessons of responsibility in order to be able to "fly" as mature adults. Rescuing our children, protecting them from becoming responsible, and preventing them from experiencing the consequences of their choices will result in crippled adults who will never "fly" with strength, confidence, and independence. In this typical example, two mothers made very different choices.

All across America on school days, children forget their lunches. It is what mothers do next that determines whether their children will experience the natural consequences of that forgetting, or will learn that it doesn't really matter if they forget because "good ol' Mom" will rescue them.

When six-year-old Ben forgot his lunch, his mother was frantic. Although she was late for an important appointment and kept others waiting, she raced to school with the all-important lunch pail.

This scenario happened repeatedly for the next two years. The school secretary even heard Ben castigate his mother on occasion: "Where have you been? I'm hungry, and my class has already gone out for lunch!" His mother was apologetic and vowed to do better next time! Of course there will be a "next time" because this mother chooses to be a rescuer and is enabling her son to continue the irresponsible "forgetting." Such behavior is certain to carry over into other areas such as returning library books on time, bringing papers home to be signed, etc.

Kimberly's mother acted quite differently when her six-year-old daughter repeatedly forgot her lunch. As a SOCCC parent, she believed in training her daughter to be a responsible person and knew that the way to do this was to make Kimberly assume the consequences for her actions. So one day Kimberly's mother did not deliver the lunch to school. She could have, but she didn't.

Kimberly survived and even thrived. The school provided milk and crackers, and willing friends shared. However, the lunch was not as good as the one from home, and Kimberly learned a valuable lesson. That afternoon Kimberly told her mother about the make-shift lunch, and how she had wanted her own lunch. When her mother asked, "What will you do next time?" Kimberly said that she would remember her lunch. "How will you remember it?" her mother then asked. Through their discussion Kimberly came to realize that putting her lunch next to the door along with her books would help her remember it in the future.

Because of her mother's action, Kimberly learned a new way of remembering her lunch (as well as other things necessary for school). She also learned that her mother considered her worthy of the responsibility of remembering her own lunch. Soon Kimberly's mom will give her more responsibility. Kimberly will be making her own lunch, and then she will be helping to decide what should be bought at the grocery store to put into the lunches. Kimberly is being allowed to mature, and is gaining more responsibility and independence as time goes by.

Which of these two children has more self-esteem? It's obvious. The child who is learning to assume responsibility is growing in capabilities, and when a person's capabilities grow, self-esteem grows also.

Allowing a child to experience the results of natural consequences is an excellent way to teach the responsibility of making good choices. However, there are times when natural consequences should not be permitted.

- *When there is danger to the child.* Parents cannot allow natural consequences of actions such as playing in the street, petting an angry dog, or getting close to a swimming pool without knowing how to swim.

- *When there is danger to another person or their property.* Parents cannot permit the natural consequences of a child injuring another person or that person's property.

- *When the results of behavior are not immediately apparent.* Although parents recognize the importance of oral hygiene, a child may not see the necessity of brushing his teeth regularly and carefully. As Grace Kelly said, "A good parent doesn't wait for teeth brushing until the child is old enough to decide for himself!"

Logical Consequences

Logical consequences do not happen naturally. They are established by the parent or authority figure and demonstrate to the child what consequences will logically follow the choice. These consequences can be either positive or negative, depending upon the choice made.

Logical consequences are set up to encourage your child to behave responsibly, and are administered in a firm, loving manner, without anger or hostility.

There are three questions you need to ask yourself before specifying a consequence. Asking these three questions will insure that the consequence is logical and will not trigger rebellion in the heart of your child.[3]

1. *Is the consequence RELATED to the behavior?*
If your child messes up the kitchen, having him clean up the kitchen is a related and logical consequence. Grounding him for a day would not be either a related or a logical consequence.

Perhaps you have a family rule that a child must eat what's on his plate before having dessert. If that rule is violated, a related, logical consequence would be to eliminate dessert at the next meal where dessert is offered. Spanking your child for disobeying the rule would not be a related, logical consequence.

2. *Is the consequence RESPECTFUL to the child?*
Screaming at your child in hasty, uncontrolled anger is not being respectful and, in time, your child will scream back.

Attacking your child with such questions as, "Why can't you ever . . .?" "How many times do I have to tell you?" and "When will you ever learn?" is demeaning and humiliating to your child. This will result in angry rebellion or withdrawal in hurt, quiet anger.

Each time you scream at your child, it is as if a poison has been injected that spreads and kills the fragile cells of self-esteem. Without healthy self-esteem, your child can't achieve his potential. Instead he will become increasingly anxious, insecure, and angry.[4] If you respect your child, he will respect you.

It is crucial to remember that a respectful consequence always takes into account the relationship between you and your child. If there are old, long-standing patterns of resentment and power-struggles, few consequences or threats will work. Your child literally loses the capacity to care. Loss of dessert, TV, play time, or other privileges mean little to an angry, hurt child. Your child will gain more satisfaction or sense of power from holding out against you at all costs than he could gain by earning a certain privilege. You must communicate love and respect in words and actions.

> *Love is the only lasting, healthy motivator in giving up one's pleasure for difficult choice making!*

3. *Is the consequence reasonable?*
It is never reasonable for a child who has not done his homework to write 25, 50, or 100 times "I will not forget to do my homework again."

It is reasonable for you to expect your child to understand what a grade will mean for the grading period, to ask the teacher if there is any way possible to make up the missing work, and to make certain that each assignment is written down in a homework notebook. In addition, if a mandatory homework time has not been established, it needs to be started immediately for the educational well-being of your child.

Logical consequences that are related, respectful, and reasonable should be agreed upon in advance of the choice by both parent and child, as this story illustrates.

Fifteen-year-old Michelle wanted to go on a weekend ski trip the following month with some of her friends. She asked her parents, assuring them there would be adequate supervision. It sounded like an extravagant idea to her parents, and they had one question: "How are you going to get the money for the trip?" Michelle had casually mentioned that the weekend would cost $200.00.

Michelle earned money through babysitting and had approximately one hundred dollars for the trip. The trip was three weeks away but she had to pay in advance. Michelle and her parents discussed the trip. No extra hundred dollars were floating around in the family, but one of the other families was willing to lend Michelle the money. She was ecstatic, but her parents were far less so, reminding her that Christmas was coming, and that it would be difficult to pay back the money and still have anything for gifts and the extras of the holiday season.

Michelle was certain it would all work out. She convinced her parents that she had the earning power through her babysitting to take care of the loan and Christmas too. Michelle and her parents agreed that the debt would have to be paid before anything else was purchased.

The ski trip was great fun, but soon it was over. Christmas and the one-hundred-dollar debt loomed on her horizon. Paying back the money took longer than Michelle thought. With Christmas less than one week away, she still hadn't paid it off.

Michelle became desperate and asked her parents to advance her some money for Christmas. They sat down with her and calmly reviewed her choice to go on the trip, her choice to accept the loan, and the agreed consequence of paying back the loan before buying anything for Christmas. She told her parents, "I'm trying as hard as I can!"

Her parents congratulated her on her conscientiousness in paying off the debt. Then they suggested she call some of the people who used her as a babysitter and let them know she was available. They also suggested she might consider making gifts of baked goods to help relieve the financial stress.

Michelle worked hard. With extra babysitting jobs, the debt was paid, she earned a little money for Christmas, and was shopping and baking on the 24th.

She was proud of herself for paying off the loan and being able to earn a little Christmas money. When her parents asked, "What would you do next time?" Michelle replied, "I've been thinking about that. The trip was fun, but so expensive. If I didn't have to borrow money, I might go, but trying to pay off the loan and get ready for Christmas was just too much. I don't want to go through that again."

Allowing children to assume the responsibility for the logical consequences of limited choices empowers them in two extremely important ways:

- *Children learn to make wise decisions*. Wisdom is the correct use of knowledge and is developed slowly and carefully as parents provide appropriate choices that include related, respectful, and responsible consequences.

- *Children develop strength of character.* As parents allow their children to endure the temporary discom-

fort of painful consequences, the children develop
inner strength. Character is being molded, chiseled,
sanded, and refined.

This invaluable combination of wisdom and strength will
serve your children well in later years as they face the
inevitable difficulties and heartaches of life. Wisdom and
strength will enable them to emerge tested and tried,
instead of disillusioned and destroyed.

It takes thought and patience to plan appropriate consequences. And it also takes a commitment to consistency.

S = Situation—A Dangerous Opportunity

O = Options—A Gamut of Possibilities

C = Choice—Power over Destiny

C = Consequences—The Law of Life

C = Consistency—The Parental Commitment

– 9 –
Consistency—
The Parental Commitment

*Without consistency,
there is no moral strength.*
OWEN

Cynthia had been successful in the world of fashion, had established her own company, and had a ready market in thousands of retail stores. She had waited until she was in her middle 30s to have children and now had three.

Meeting her for lunch was quite an experience. I (Pat) remembered when she used to be organized and always punctual. But this time, she was nearly fifteen minutes late. Instead of being flawlessly groomed, she appeared hastily thrown together. She plopped herself down and announced to me, "Life is difficult, but parenting is more than difficult—it's exhausting. Running my own company was a game in comparison to being a mom!"

Cynthia's Story

Cynthia proceeded to share the exploits of her children. "Ray is two, and everything is 'No!' If it's something I know he wants, and I ask him, he still says 'No!' The television blasts all day, no matter how many times I tell the kids to turn it off. The five- and eight-year-olds race through the house with carefree abandon. Something falling and breaking barely gets their attention. The house should be declared a disaster area. No one picks up anything but me, and when I ask them to do something, it's as if they are deaf. I can't get them to do anything around the house. The minute I sit them down, they're up and sneaking out. And do you know why I'm late? They hid the keys to the car. Can you believe it? What one doesn't think of, the other two do. . . . You've been taking care of other people's children for years, plus raising your own. How can you stand it?"

I asked her a question in return. "Do you really want to learn how to parent, or would you rather complain?"

Cynthia looked at me quizzically for a minute, realizing the question was not a simple one. Then she asked, "What will it take?"

"I can give you the principles you need," I answered. "After that, it's up to you. Whether you succeed or fail will depend on only one thing—a commitment to consistency. Knowing the principles is good, using them is better, but applying the approach plus a commitment to consistency is best, and will insure your success as a parent!"

Cynthia was quiet for a long moment, then responded, "I'm ready, and so is my husband. We can't go on like this any longer. Let us have it!"

And so they began to learn how to become SOCCC parents. Gradually, they learned about giving appropriate choices and consequences and began to apply these principles in their home.

Slowly a transformation occurred. The children were delighted to have choices instead of being told what to do and being screamed at, and they made the necessary adjustment to the responsibility of consequences. When Cynthia and her husband conscientiously and consistently applied the SOCCC principles, the power struggles faded and then disappeared.

Several lunches later, Cynthia asked, "When do we let up? It takes a lot of work to think up the appropriate choices, and then think up consequences that are related, respectful, and responsible."

"Of course it's a lot of work!" I laughed. "Who said parenting was easy? Your commitment to consistency must continue for your parenting to be successful. Children are secure when they have boundaries and know what is expected. They grow responsible when they know what the consequences of their choices will be, both positive and negative."

Cynthia sighed, "That's what I knew you'd say. O.K. It's working so well, I don't want to change anything. I'll keep on keepin' on!"

Amanda's Story

Amanda was different. Although she said she and her husband wanted to have control in their home and teach their children to be responsible, she didn't mean it. Each time suggestions were made, she would say, "But . . ." The situations she encountered in her home were common—defiance and rebellion resulting in screaming and frustration. She refused to offer choices, but continued giving ultimatums. Instead of allowing the children to assume the consequences, she would berate and rescue.

When Amanda's teenage son, Kevin, wanted money for a car, she told him he would have to earn the money. "Your father and I have done enough for you. We have bought you everything you've needed, and then some. We've always been there for you. It's high time you did something on your own. We can't afford to get you a car. You will have to get a job and keep a job—and that's final."

As usual, Kevin procrastinated. He talked about getting a job but did nothing. Instead of accepting that as his choice and letting Kevin assume the consequence, Amanda "arranged" to have him start a paper route. "You're plenty old enough. It will make you responsible. Don't you dare disappoint me after all I went through to get this for you."

Whose job was it? Amanda got it for her son, it wasn't Kevin's choice, and he was not too interested in delivering papers. She set her alarm "just to make sure" he got up, which he did with great effort and annoyance. When the weather was too cold or too stormy, Amanda drove the car. After several months of this, accompanied by her endless lectures on responsibility, Kevin quit. Amanda was furious. "How could you do this to me—after all I've done to make you successful? What are you going to do now? If you fail at delivering papers, you will fail at everything. I give up."

Instead of being consistent with choices and consequences, Amanda could be counted on for futile and destructive outbursts of frustration. No wonder she was continually upset and disappointed. If only she had let Kevin get his own job or suffer the consequence of not getting one at all, he would have been more interested in working. If only she had let Kevin be responsible for doing the work instead of rescuing under the guise of "helping," he would have gained respect for himself—and for her. If only Amanda had stopped lecturing and allowed her son the opportunity to make choices and reap the consequences, he would have grown in maturity. She could have saved herself—and Kevin—a great deal of frustration.

Growing Oak Trees

Before James Garfield was President of the United States, he was President of Hiram College in Ohio. A father of one of the freshman came to see him with a complaint. "My son feels you are too strict. The discipline is too rigid, and the classes are too difficult. Can't you offer some shortcuts for the students to make their lives better and the work easier?"

James Garfield looked at the father and said, "It depends on what you want to grow. If you want to grow an oak tree, it takes a long time. The tree must grow strong enough to withstand the heat of the summer, the winds and rain of autumn, the severe cold and storms of winter, as well as the surprises of spring. If you want to grow squash, it only takes a few weeks, and then it is gone." [1]

With a continuing commitment to consistency, SOCCC parents grow children with roots of responsibility and wings of independence.[2] Although the principles of choice and consequences do not change, the application of the principles varies with each age and stage of your child's development. This requires flexibility. Sam, your two-year-old has different needs from Laura, your twelve-year-old. Because Sarah is older, she should have more choices and therefore greater responsibility. You must adjust the choices and consequences with flexibility and good judgment.

The Symbol

In the SOCCC parenting symbol, we have now discussed each of the letters: S = Situation—A Dangerous Opportunity; O = Options—A Gamut of Possibilities; C = Choice—Power over Destiny; C = Consequences—The Law of Life;

C = Consistency—The Parental Commitment. In our SOCCC logo, we have surrounded the situation, options, choice, and consequences with the C of consistency. Why is this final C so important?

Consistency is the mortar that secures the SOCCC approach into a complete parenting plan. If we were to build a brick home, we would design carefully, organize the materials, and assemble them according to the plan. Leaving out the mortar would be ridiculous. The house would not last the first storm. So it is with childrearing. The SOCCC approach is excellent—and it works—but the parental commitment to consistency is essential for making it work through all the parenting years.

In Part III, we'll discuss how SOCCC is applied through each stage of your child's development.

Part III

It to 'em—Through the Years

*Many of life's circumstances
are created by three basic choices:
the disciplines you choose to keep, the
people you choose to be with, and the
laws you choose to obey.*
CHARLES MILLHUFF

– 10 –
Infants and Toddlers
(Birth–3)

Teaching decision making to children varies amazingly according to their ages. In this section, we will give you examples of dilemmas and choices and show how you can guide your child to choose wisely. The questions and suggestions at the end of each dilemma will help you learn the final C of the SOCCC approach—consistency.

Dilemma #1

Three-week-old Brian awakens at 2:00 a.m. His stomach is empty, and his hunger pains tell him so. Furthermore, his diaper is soggy and he feels chilly. His parents are sound asleep. Brian "chooses" to cry, and his cry is the only means by which he can say, "Help! I'm miserable!"

While three-week old Brian is not actively thinking, "I'm going to scream out so Mom or Dad will take care of me," he is reacting to a life situation. (Many people go through life making reactive choices.) It is Brian's parents who must use their thinking ability to teach him.

Situation   Baby is hungry, wet, and cold. He craves
                  attention.

Options   These are not yet understood by Brian,
                  but he will learn them from his parents'
                  mode of handling him. If they respond to
                  him lovingly, restore his comfort, and
                  refuse to encourage his nocturnal habits
                  by playing with him, he will learn to go
                  back to sleep and, gradually, to sleep
                  through the night.

Choice   Babies learn to cry less and trust more
                  when parents are consistent, gentle, and
                  strong. The development of trust, then, is
                  fundamental to learning to make con-
                  scious choices later on.

Consequences   The result of Brian's crying will teach
                  him what to do next time. If his parents
                  are very slow to respond but eventually
                  do so, Brian will believe (experience) that
                  loud, unceasing noise will get results. So
                  he will learn to "hang in there," keep up
                  his demands, and finally get the payoff.

Consistency   If Brian's parents are consistent in the
                  way they respond to his cries and in the
                  length of time it takes them to reach him,
                  Brian will know what to expect. This
                  early training for both parent and child
                  will pay big dividends later.

As you consider how to react to your infant (or recall how you once did), you can quickly see what you are teaching him or her. If you don't like what you see, try these simple steps:

1. Try to imagine yourself as a baby. What would you need and how would you like your parents to respond?

2. Keep in mind what you, as an adult, need in terms of rest, taking care of other duties, and enjoyment of your baby.

3. Plan your response to be efficient, loving, and even happy—teaching your child to trust you and making obedience a choice he or she will be more willing to make later on. A child will sacrifice his selfish interests and wishes to please the parent he loves and feels safe with.

4. Perform your response as consistently as possible to build the strongest bonds of trust, respect, and security with your child (even when you don't feel like it!).

Dilemma #2

Even at one, Melanie's brown eyes flashed angrily. She wanted the brightly printed music books in her mother's rack. The pictures were pretty and her past experience with old magazines told her that the sound of tearing paper was fun. She felt very much in charge of life when she ripped up the newspaper.

But here was Mother saying emphatically, "No, Melanie!" She was even blocking Melanie's access to those lovely pages. Perhaps, if she just waited a bit, Mom would go away. Mom, however, didn't leave! She stayed right there, and her voice said, "I mean business, Melanie! It's time you learn to choose to stay within your limits. You may *not* play with my expensive sheet music!"

Situation

This situation is more complex than Brian's hunger pains. Melanie wants to explore, to learn, to experience—and Mom wants her to do all those things. Expensive music, however, is not for tearing and tasting (what any one-year-old is likely to do with it). It's time for Melanie to learn to choose—to stay away from something she wants.

Options

The options are simple—to persist in playing with the music or to stay away from it. Mother is the real decision maker, but, by choice, she will teach Melanie wisdom or foolishness. Mom's options are these:

- She can indulge her child, let Melanie destroy the expensive items, and replace them.
- She can put the sheets out of reach, postponing the eventual task of teaching Melanie to respect proper limits.
- She can schedule the time to teach Melanie to respect other people's property.

Our recommendation, of course, is that Mom use the last option by:

- Firmly, seriously (but not angrily) restraining Melanie every time she reaches for the forbidden item saying, "No!"
- Staying with this struggle until Mom wins. (Even if it takes all afternoon!)
- Testing the genuineness of Melanie's mastery of this vital lesson. Melanie's mom might step out of Melanie's range of vision and see if she still refrains from touching the item. Only then has this basic step been learned.
- If Melanie reverts to her old efforts to grab the music, Mom must repeat the teaching experience.

Once this lesson is mastered, later choices will become easier to make correctly.

Choice   Both Mother and Melanie have choices to make. How Melanie learns, at one year, is determined by the action and manner her mother chooses to employ. Firm, consistent, tenacious teaching will pay off well in Melanie's learning to live with limits.

Consequences   While Melanie was in the process of learning to accept limits, the consequen-

ces of her repeated choice to try to grab
the music were unpleasant. Both Mother
and Melanie would have liked for her to
be able to explore and experience life. But
in this case, that wish would have been
too expensive. So the negative consequences prevailed. Once the lesson was
learned, however, Mom could enthusiastically express her pride in her child's
achievement.

Consistency   By her firm and loving discipline,
Melanie's mother is setting the imprint
of later habit patterns in choosing.

Dilemma #3

Danny, trying desperately to look alert, was nonetheless
getting very sleepy. It was past naptime, and he was
playing with his brightly colored building blocks. His wise
mother set the kitchen timer and reminded him, "Danny,
when the timer rings, you must pick up your blocks. Then
we'll read a story before your nap."

Danny, a bright and independent boy, has a choice to
make. He may refuse to pick up the toys and throw a fit, or
he can pick them up and enjoy the promised story. There's
a third possibility, too. Danny can see if Mom really means
the command or if she will forget or even do the task for
him.

How vital it is, at this early age, for mothers to be
absolutely consistent. Children *almost never* like to stop
playing to do something less fun. When parents fail to
follow through every time, the child's choices become too

complicated. They may get the extra play time but earn Mom's disapproval. Sometimes they may feel the disapproval is worth it because they get their way and have a bit more fun time. If the love between mother and child is secure, however, the child will be far more likely to sacrifice his wishes for her approval and pride.

Please be aware, again and again, of the power of a loving relationship in creating the best possible climate for good choosing! This power must never be used in a manipulative manner to coerce wise choosing, but without it all other techniques will fall short sooner or later.

Eighteen-month-old Danny, then, faces this predicament:

Situation   As already mentioned, Danny faces giving up pleasure for duty. His fatigue makes him grouchy, and that probably prompts Mother to be impatient. He may not want to be compliant and agreeable at all!

Options   The options are listed above. At a year and a half, Danny is still reacting more than clearly choosing, but he has a budding awareness of some power to choose how he will react.

Choice   Choosing, at Danny's age, is crucially related to previous experiences. If Mother has allowed him to get by without obeying or if she forgets to follow through when the timer goes off, Danny will have a difficult time knowing how to decide.

Consequences The consequences are of vital importance to Danny's learning to choose. If Mom says, "Danny, I saw by your face that you wanted to keep on playing, but I watched you when the timer buzzed. You started to pick up your blocks. I'm really proud of you for that! Let's cuddle in the rocking chair while I read to you about the pokey little puppy."

With such a response, how can Danny lose? And how can he and Mom fail to grow ever closer in a loving and trusting relationship?

Consistency The best motivator to choosing right is love—and that's what Danny's mother is proving to him by her consistency even in small things like naps and picking up toys.

If you have a small child, these examples can be useful. But we know many of you have missed this golden opportunity—your children are older. How can you recap your losses and correct possible mistakes? Here are some suggestions:

1. Tell your older child—even your teenager (at the right time and in the proper mood)—stories about those early years. Frankly describe the events you mishandled and tell them how sorry you are for whatever pain that caused.

2. Next, devise a plan to change old habits, forming new and better ones. Seek your child's input as to what he or she would like from you that will make future decisions easier.

3. Write a reminder to yourself and ask your child to tell you if you backslide. It takes plenty of effort and time to form new habits.

4. Stick with it! It's well worth it.

Dilemma #4

Decision making in childhood truly explodes at two. Most Twos talk quite well, understand a great deal, and are struggling heroically to find out what they can do and just who they are. Making choices is extremely important.

We strongly recommend that parents think carefully about choices they can realistically offer a child at this age. A common mistake is to offer too many choices. Another is to become entangled in arguments about those choices.

For example, Anne's father asks, "What do you want for breakfast today?" Because Anne happens to love ice cream, she promptly replies, "I want ice cream!" You can imagine the battle that ensues. Without realizing it, Dad has set up a struggle no one will really win.

He may further engage Anne in battle by saying, "You know we don't have ice cream for breakfast!" And Anne is likely to scream, "But I WANT ice cream!" It's small wonder that people describe this stage as the "Terrible Twos" rather than the truly "Terrific Twos."

How does our SOCCC routine apply to Anne and her father?

Situation   Dad wants to please Anne and prepare a breakfast she will enjoy. He just doesn't realize how simply and concretely Twos think. His mental picture is Cheerios, or scrambled eggs and toast. But he fails to describe those possibilities. Anne has too much freedom to choose and she does what any self-respecting Two would do. She holds out for the one food she really wants and can't have.

Options   At two, children can usually see and handle only two options. It would have worked better for Dad to ask clearly, "Anne, do you want cereal or an egg this morning?" Or, "Anne, you may have your egg scrambled or hard-boiled. Which would you like?" Such possibilities are clear to a Two.

Choice   Even limited choices may be difficult for Anne. If she is in a cross mood, she may choose a scrambled egg and then refuse to eat it. This behavior certainly ping-pongs back to Dad and his next decision! He may decide to punish Anne for her rudeness, beg her to eat the egg, or try to force it into her mouth.

Consequences If, however, she feels good, is hungry, and likes eggs, she may choose to eat it nicely and even ask for more. Dad may take this positive action for granted and not even respond, or he may realize such good behavior deserves a compliment and smile of approval.

For Anne, then, the consequence depends on her attitude and her decision, as well as her dad's response to her:

- If Anne refuses to eat her breakfast, Dad may react positively by saying, "Anne, I should have told you we're only choosing from breakfast foods at breakfast time. Let's choose again: Are you hungry for Cheerios or scrambled eggs?" No one loses in this transaction, and Anne is still offered an opportunity to choose.

- If Anne stages an angry fit because she can't have ice cream, Dad can give in and let her have ice cream just to restore peace; he can spank her, making her even more angry, or he can yell at her and try to force her to eat. Later, Dad would feel sorry and Anne would feel frightened or angry. No one wins much with this sort of interaction.

- If Anne is compliant, gives up her wish and pleases Dad, they may get through the day okay. But Anne may be learning to give in too easily—a sort of puppet who tries to please whoever pulls the strings.

Consistency   Anne's father has a lot of options. He can choose to be consistent (probably the harder immediate choice because it will involve denying Anne the breakfast of ice cream she wants) or take the easy way out by giving in to his daughter's demands (which will be damaging to Anne in the long run). What would you do?

Dilemma #5

Gary was just finishing breakfast. He had learned to say, "Please!" and was asked to say it after each meal before he was lifted out of the high chair.

Gary and his mother had chatted during breakfast, then had "read" an object picture book together. Now his mother asked, "Are you ready to get down?" Gary nodded his head. "Say 'Please,' and you may get down." Gary did not respond. His mother asked, "Are you ready to say 'Please?'" Gary shook his head. "Then you are not ready to get out of your high chair."

His mother did not say anything else, but began to do the morning dishes. After a couple of minutes, she asked again, "Are you ready to say 'Please'?" Gary was emphatic—"*No!*" Mom responded again, "Then you are not ready to get out of your high chair."

There was more silence as Mom completed washing the morning dishes. Several minutes had gone by. "Now are you ready to say 'Please'?" Gary was still emphatic—"*No!*"

What a drag! What should Gary's mother do? In her heart, she wanted to let him down. His diaper needed changing—badly—and she wanted to get going with the rest of the day. But in her heart, she also realized that this act of simple defiance was in reality a power struggle and, if not handled properly, would be the first of many more. She made a decision to stick it out, and Gary was given the choice and the consequence.

"Gary," his mother said in an even voice, "You know how to say 'Please.' When you say 'Please,' you get down. As soon as you say 'Please,' you may get out of your high chair and play. You may not get down and play until you have said 'Please.' Do you understand?" Gary nodded. "Are you ready to say 'Please'?" Gary shook his head. "I have other things to do in the house," his mother stated. "I will come back very soon and see if you are ready to say 'Please.' " Then she left the kitchen.

What have I started? she asked herself. *What if he doesn't say "Please" for the rest of the day? I can see the headlines now—UNFIT MOTHER LEAVES CHILD IN HIGH CHAIR FOR 24 HOURS!* She nearly shivered. *Oh God,* she prayed, *Please let Gary say "Please,"* then smiled at the ridiculousness of the situation. *They never told me about this part of parenting,* she thought. She felt somewhat guilty and ineffective but remained firm in her resolve to follow through.

Quickly she went back into the kitchen. "What are you going to say, Gary?" No response. "Gary, your diaper needs changing. If you do not say 'Please,' I will take you out of the high chair, change your diaper, put on clean play clothes, and then put you back until you are ready to say, 'Please.' As soon as you say 'Please,' you may get down and play. Are you ready to play?" Gary nodded. *(Thank God,* his mom thought, *Now we are getting somewhere.)* "Are you ready to say 'Please'?" Gary shook his head. *(Nuts! He's as stubborn as I am.)* "Then you are not going to be able to play. Remember, you need to say 'Please'!"

Believe it or not, this went on for another half hour. Gary's diaper and clothes were changed, and he was put back into the high chair. All the while his mother was thinking, *What am I going to do with this child? If he's like this now, what does the future hold?*

"Do you want to play, Gary?" He gave a vigorous, "Yes!" "Do you know what to say?" He nodded. "As soon as you say it, you may get down." A long moment of silence passed. Then a weak, "P- please" was heard. His mother was elated! *(Thank God! No "UNFIT MOTHER" headlines.)* "Now you may get down, and play!" She helped Gary down, and he toddled off to play. His mother sat down, sighed with obvious relief, and wondered what the next meal would bring.

Guess who the mother was? *Me (Pat)!* And I'm pleased to tell you that incident was the first and last of its kind with my son. He found out early that I said what I meant, that I meant what I said the first time, and that I could be counted on to follow through—even when it was tough and took a long time!

Let's put this dilemma into our SOCCC framework:

Situation   Gary was in his high chair and ready to get down and play.

Options	He could say "Please" and get down or not say "Please" and stay in the high chair.
Choice	He made a choice not to say "Please" and to stay in the chair.
Consequences	He stayed in the chair until he was ready to say, "Please."
Consistency	I gave him the choice and the consequence and was consistent, even though I thought the situation was ridiculous. I felt somewhat guilty and, for a while, ineffective. However, I followed through without giving up and rescuing my son, losing my temper, or cajoling. The choice was always his to stay or to get down!

What if I had become impatient with the lack of immediate response and given in to my child, saying, "Well, I'm going to let you get down this time, but I hope you've learned your lesson and won't ever do this again!" You can be certain that Gary would have learned a valuable lesson—the one who holds out is the winner!

Dilemma #6

Rebecca was an adorable child, nearly two years old, who had already developed a liking for beautiful things and felt the urge to look and touch. Her mother realized she needed to explore and learn and allowed her to touch certain things in each room in the house. However, there were other things that Rebecca could look at but not touch.

On a table in the living room was a small porcelain basket of flowers. Rebecca had taken a great liking to the arrangement and, even before she could talk, would begin to gurgle whenever she got close to the piece.

Now that she could walk, her mother watched carefully on this particular day as she neared the porcelain. Rebecca's hand went out. Her mother said "No! You may look at it with your eyes, but you may not touch it!" Rebecca's hand drew back ever so slightly, then went out again toward the porcelain. The mother repeated, "No!" This time Rebecca's hand did not draw back, but merely paused mid-air for an instant, then continued forward toward the porcelain. Her mother thought for a moment, *If she won't listen, then she must feel!* and flicked Rebecca's hand. The hand drew back instantly. Rebecca looked up at her mother, incredulous that someone who claimed to love her could inflict pain.

Rebecca recovered her composure, looked at the porcelain, looked at her mother, and put out her hand. "No!" came the word from her mother. "You may look at it with your eyes, but you may not touch it." Rebecca was not convinced. Her hand went out, quickly this time, toward the porcelain. "No!" her mother said again, this time with feeling. Rebecca kept the hand moving and received another "No!" and a flick on the hand.

At this point, Rebecca toddled away to safer ground, touched some of the objects in the room she was both permitted and encouraged to explore, and received her mother's blessing. But Rebecca still had the porcelain on her mind. She glanced at it from time to time, then played with the acceptable items.

After a few minutes, Rebecca headed back to the table where the forbidden porcelain lay. With absolutely no hesitancy, she reached out with determination. "No!" came her mother's response. "You may not touch the basket." Rebecca's body language was clear. She was disgusted with all these nos. She gave her mother a look of disdain and went for the porcelain. The mother was consistent. "No!" was the response, accompanied by a flick on Rebecca's adorable little hand.

Frustration was the word, for both mother and daughter. The daughter was frustrated that she could not have what she wanted. The mother was frustrated that Rebecca kept on wanting what was strictly forbidden, when she had provided so many other wonderful things to touch and to handle.

At this point, Mother wondered, *Perhaps this is just too much to ask of any small child. She cannot be detoured easily. Maybe I should just put the porcelain piece away until this stage passes, and put it back when she is older. It would be a lot easier for both of us!* But something inside of her said, *She needs to learn that she can't have everything she wants, and she needs to learn that a little at a time. Also, this is my house. I should be able to enjoy the things I like, and she needs to learn self-control. That's it. I'm leaving the porcelain on the table!*

While the mother was thinking her thoughts, Rebecca was deciding that life was really not worth living until she touched the porcelain. Thus she would dedicate herself to the task. The lines were drawn. Both mother and daughter knew what they wanted.

For the next several days, the living-room scenes were a series of hands reaching out, eliciting a resounding "No!" often accompanied by a flick, and then a cry of frustration from Rebecca. The mother held herself together, crying only in private!

Her mother wondered, *Will this child ever stop trying to touch the porcelain? Will my entire life be spent saying, "No!" to something that doesn't really matter anyway?* Then she reassured herself, *It's the principle I'm working for—a child who can learn self-control. She'll certainly need it as the years go by. How many things have I wanted that weren't good for me, that I had to say, "No!" to?*

Almost a week later, the mother's efforts were rewarded. Rebecca came near the porcelain, looked at it longingly, looked at her mother, smiled, and said "No!", then moved to touch something acceptable. *Hooray!* the mother breathed with conviction.

Several days later, a couple came over for dinner. They also had a toddler at home. The woman walked into the house, looked over the living room and announced, "You can tell this isn't a house for children!" At the time, the mother had Rebecca, an older son, and an infant daughter. The mother was silent, but she and her husband had many laughs over the thoughtless remark.

Rebecca was always welcome in people's homes and shops as a little girl because she could keep her hands off objects and look but not touch until she was given something to handle. She is a teenager now, still loves flowers, takes painting classes and a class in floral arranging, and enjoys going to museums and art galleries.

The other mother's child? He is now also in his teens and has had continuing problems in self-control over the years. He was never expected to learn responsibility and control slowly, step by step in the early years, and has found it next to impossible as a teen.

The dilemma can be put into the SOCCC approach:

Situation	Rebecca was in the living room, wanting to touch the porcelain basket of flowers.
Options	She could play with the acceptable things or attempt to touch the porcelain and hear "No!" from her mother and receive a flick on her hand.
Choice	Rebecca chose to continue to try to touch the porcelain.
Consequences	Repeated "No!"s from her mother, as well as flicks on the hand.
Consistency	Because Rebecca's mother was consistent over a period of time in the behavior she accepted from her daughter, her child behaved differently from other children.

How very essential it is to give children the set of choices they can manage and then help them learn by the consequences how to make good decisions more and more. Honest but kind feedback will help children understand how to incorporate experience with information in choosing well.

Teaching choices to any two-year-old is a challenge demanding one's best in patience, firmness, gentleness, and humor!

– 11 –
Young Children
(Ages 3–5)

Most three-year-olds are able to communicate well. They have quite a vocabulary, and they can listen and discuss many ideas with others. They are capable of a great many choices and can incorporate a range of outcomes into their thinking. Furthermore, they are much more positive and charming in their attitudes and behaviors than two-year-olds are.

Their scope of choices also broadens. While Twos can usually decide to obey their parents or rebel, Threes must decide how to treat peers and what to do in play activities. They employ a range of fantasies that involve a great deal of rather complex thinking.

We see very little difference between three- and four-year-olds. Fours are, however, typically full of questions about anything and *everything!*

In order to see how three–five-year-olds can develop socially, emotionally, intellectually, and spiritually, let's take a look at these dilemmas, using the SOCCC approach.

SOCIAL CHOICES

Dilemma #1

Debbie awoke one sunny morning all smiles. She cheerfully ate her breakfast, did not annoy her little brother by teasing, and began to play independently with her toys.

Joan, her next-door neighbor, knocked on the door and wanted to play. Debbie quickly included her in the activity. Debbie's mom, observing quietly from the next room, couldn't believe it! All of Debbie's actions were quite different from a few weeks ago. Her mom realized that just last month, Debbie had turned three. Who could ever believe that such dramatic changes could occur with reaching a milestone like a birthday!

But it's true. At about three years of age, children usually seem to figure out who they are; they learn to live much more happily with rules, and their minds are capable of creative functions that are often amazing. This third year, then, becomes an important one in teaching good choices.

Let's peek in on Debbie and Joan. In spite of a great start at playing together, trouble is brewing. Joan wants to put a pink dress on the doll, and Debbie insists on a blue one. Joan wants to pretend they are taking the baby to a sitter, and Debbie wants to take her out for a ride in the toy stroller. There are choices to be made. Debbie has already learned to give in to her baby brother at times, while Joan is an only child, accustomed to having her way.

Situation

Clearly, the situation involves a difference of opinion about specific play direction. Each child wants a different choice. All too likely, Debbie will give in and Joan will get her way.

Options

With Mother's guidance, the two girls may decide to take turns choosing outfits and play activities. She might insist that Debbie be a good hostess and allow Joan to choose, or she might insist that Joan must let Debbie do it her way. What Mother does at this point is crucial to the eventual direction Debbie will take and, to a much lesser degree, Joan as well.

In clarifying options, remember that there are always several possibilities. Some are intolerable, others are mediocre, but one is usually clearly the best. How you go about teaching your three-year-old to see these and organize them will give her tools for all of her life—good or bad. Being a considerate hostess must be balanced with a sense of fairness between friends. If you recognize that giving in too much creates passivity and resentment, you'll be better able to help

your child give in at some point. And that
will be very good for your child, as well as
her friends.

Choice
At three, few children have either the
wisdom or experience to make smart
choices all the time. But they learn by
trying. Mother needs to sit down gently
with Debbie and Joan and explain,
"Girls, I heard you disageeing about what
you will play. It's okay to disagree sometimes. Let me teach you how to choose
fun activities to play together!" Mom may
then list the options and ask the girls to
choose which they will decide on first. At
this point, Mother needs to forget that
Debbie is her daughter while Joan is not;
she must treat them as equals if the
outcome is to work.

Consequences
If the girls decide to argue and be selfish,
it is likely one will quit playing, and both
will have a miserable time. If one or the
other gives in, they will continue to play,
but at the expense of healthy respect for
each other and themselves. If they agree
to take turns, they can play happily with
good self-esteem and respect for the
other.

Consistency
Mother should stand by, leaving the girls
space to choose, and then giving clear
feedback regarding the consequences.

> How blessed Debbie and Joan are to have
> such a coach!

Each of you can also be a championship coach!

Dilemma #2

Jackie and Kirsten were friends. Although they were not
neighbors, their two daughters played together whenever
possible. Both had talked about preschool as a possibility
for enrichment, socialization, and as a way of introducing
the girls to the concept of school. Kirsten was a SOCCC
parent; Jackie thought she was.

When Kirsten's daughter turned four, she decided to look
for a preschool. Jackie said she wanted to go with her, so
they visited schools together. After finding one that offered
a stimulating environment with kind, loving, yet firm
teachers, they took their daughters for a visit.

Kirsten talked to her daughter about going to preschool—how long she would be there, what she would be
doing, what would be expected of her—and then asked if
she would like to go.

Jackie didn't prepare her daughter. She merely asked,
"Do you want to go to school with your best friend?" Both
girls were excited and were enrolled for three mornings a
week.

On the first day of school, Kirsten's daughter went into
school happily, eager to play and learn. But Jackie's
daughter hung back, holding onto her mother, seeming
insecure and fearful. This same scene was reenacted daily.

On one particular morning, the teacher advised Jackie
to leave. Jackie was somewhat reluctant, and said in an
accusing tone of voice, "She doesn't want to go to school

anymore. She liked it at first. I wonder what has happened?"

The teacher assured her, "Your daughter is just fine and has a wonderful day after you leave."

Jackie and her daughter went through a very long kissing and hugging routine. As Jackie hesitatingly walked toward the door, her daughter ran after her, threw her little arms around her mother, and clung. This was too much for Jackie. Her eyes became moist, and she said to the teacher, "See what I mean? She just doesn't like it here."

The teacher continued to encourage her to leave. So did Kirsten: "Come on, Jackie. It's the only way."

Then Jackie had an idea. "Maybe it would help if I could stay—just for today." The teacher assured Jackie that after the separation problem was taken care of, she could come and visit for as long as she wanted. Jackie cried, "I just can't leave my baby unhappy like this! She needs me. I knew she wasn't ready for school, and this proves it. You can go home with Mommy, sweetheart, and we'll do something fun together." The little girl, still upset and crying, left with her mother.

Kirsten shook her head. Her daughter came looking for her friend. "She won't be able to come again to school," her mother explained gently.

The little girl was curious. "Why, Mommy?"

Kirsten replied, "She and her mommy are not as ready for school as you and I are, dear."

Her daughter acknowledged with an "Oh! I'm a big girl, aren't I, Mommy?"

"You certainly are," her mother assured her. "Have a wonderful morning. I'll be back at lunchtime."

"Okay, Mommy! Bye!"

This situation is common in preschools and, almost always, is the mother's problem, not the child's. For any one of a variety of reasons, the mother feels guilty about leaving the child in school and is not ready to separate from her child for a regular period of time each week. The child merely responds to the emotions of the mother and actually becomes a victim of the mother's fears and anxieties.

Let's put this in the SOCCC framework:

Situation	After looking at various preschools, two mothers and their daughters decide to attend a certain preschool three mornings a week.
Options	Preschool attendance is an option. Both mothers need to think carefully through the responsibilities of attendance *for their daughters, individually.*
Choice	Kirsten decided to enroll her daughter in preschool. Carefully, she explained to her daughter what would happen at preschool, how long she would be there, etc.
	Jackie decided to enroll her daughter in preschool also. However, instead of thinking carefully about how preschool would affect her daughter, she went along with Kirsten's decision out of friendship. Jackie didn't prepare her daughter for her preschool experience.

Consequences   Because Kirsten's daughter knew what would be happening to her, she adjusted to preschool life admirably. This new phase in her life made her feel "like a big girl" and helped her develop some emotional distance from her mother (which is part of the growing-up process).

Jackie's daughter, on the other hand, was a sobbing, fearful child, who didn't know what would happen to her when her mother left.

Consistency   Jackie wasn't consistent in her behavior as a parent. She could have taken this moment to repair some of the damage her earlier decision (not to tell her daughter about school) had done by giving her daughter consistent love with firm discipline.

But that's not what happened. The mother continued to protect her "baby," projecting blame on others (the teacher for instance) for her daughter's adjustment problem, and whisking her off toward the "safe" haven of home.

On the other hand, because Kirsten was a consistent, loving parent, her daughter felt safe to learn and enjoy playing with other children away from home.

Which child do you think will be better able to tackle new concepts, people, and places as she experiences the years of elementary school, junior high, and high school?

EMOTIONAL
CHOICES

Dilemma #1

For most of us, our ability to choose how we will act, react, and feel is a hard concept to grasp. Taking charge of our emotions requires the greatest possible strength! By "taking charge" we don't mean repressing or suppressing. Rather, we mean facing emotions honestly and squarely, admitting how we feel—angry, sad, scared, worried, excited, loving.

Identifying those emotions is not enough. Next, those feelings must be traced back to their cause and the inner needs that accompany them. Once we can identify the source of the emotion, we can make a choice regarding the timing and mode of expressing it.

Practicing these skills can keep anyone out of really tense or risky interactions.

Take this situation for example.

Situation   Sarah is three years old—at the peak point of craving her independence. While walking with Aunt Eva to the store, she slips on some gravel and falls, skinning her knees painfully.

Aunt Eva stops, helps Sarah up, tries to clean off the debris, and attempts to comfort her. To her amazement, Sarah becomes angry, yells at her to "leave me alone!" and refuses all offers of help.

At three, Sarah is unable to recognize the element of choice. She is embarrassed at what must seem babyish, cannot admit her need for help, and covers her pain with anger.

Sarah is hurt physically, but, much more importantly, her pride is hurt. Most likely, Aunt Eva has no idea what's going on. She may be hurt by Sarah's apparently rude rejection of her help.

Options

Aunt Eva may scold and shame Sarah for her "rudeness."

Or she may stop and think, putting herself in her niece's place, guessing at the "cover up." She may then explain Sarah's dilemma and point out the facts: it was the gravel that made her fall, not the fact that she is little; that she is very brave to want to handle her own pain; and that all of us, even grown-ups, sometimes need help. When she is ready for help in cleaning up the scratches, she may ask for it.

Such options obviously offer a child respect and confidence; the understanding heart of Aunt Eva will cement a loving relationship and even this painful experience can end in increased security for Sarah.

Choice   At three Sarah is unlikely to use words to explain her choice. Instead, she will act it out. For example, she will try to finish the errand bravely but may burst into tears when they reach a private spot. That is the time for comfort and emotional Band-Aids.

Consequences Sarah's fall is really coincidental. All children (and many adults) fall. But it's her reaction to the fall that offers consequences. And those, in this case, depend upon the response of the adult.

Consistency   Calm, carefully chosen reactions can enable a child's trust to grow, maintain her dignity, and help her know what to do if she is hurt again.

Dilemma #2

Andy was a four-year-old, freckle-faced bundle of charm. He was extremely well coordinated and moved quickly with a ball or a bicycle, but was very slow when it came to getting dressed and leaving the house.

This was an ongoing point of contention between Andy and his mother, especially since she had recently taken a part-time job and had to get Andy to preschool and herself to work on time.

This dawdling is absolutely maddening! his mother thought to herself. *There must be something I can do to make it stop!*

Andy was particularly negligent regarding his shoes. They might be *anywhere*—except in his closet, of course. That was the only place guaranteed *not* to contain shoes.

On this particular morning, the mother was nearly ready to leave. Andy had dressed (except for his shoes), finished breakfast, and was playing. One look at his stocking feet was enough to bring steam out of his mother's ears. *Control*, she thought angrily. *I must keep control, and not say anything I will regret. What to do . . . what to do . . . ?*

She barely stopped herself from screaming, "I've told you a MILLION times to get your shoes on BEFORE you start playing. You have TWO minutes to find your shoes, and if they aren't on in two minutes, you're going to school without them!"

Then she pictured the inevitable in her mind's eye. The two minutes were up, and still, the shoes were not found. She would have to force a screaming, kicking, angry son into the car, probably shutting the door on his hand in the process. The hysterical sobbing would continue all the way to school, accompanied by her screams of how many times she had told him, etc. Arriving at school, he would have to be forced out of the car, still hysterical and unable to function. The entire school would hear the screeching, see the boy without shoes, and every parent and teacher would be talking about "that woman who let her son come to school without shoes!"

Andy's mother shook her head—still not knowing what to do, she looked at her watch in dismay. Time had not stood still during her fantasy side trip. She had to get out of the house. Then an idea came. Andy loved to wear his tennis shoes, once they were found and on his feet. They were new, and he was certain he could run faster than ever with them. He called them his "racing shoes!" But he was not too fond of his slip-on dress shoes, which were kept in a box on the top shelf of his closet. (Surprisingly enough, both Andy and his mom knew where that pair was!)

Hmm . . . , she thought to herself. *Yes, that is it—a logical consequence that is related, responsible, and respectful!* "Andy," she said in a firm tone of voice. "We are leaving the house in two minutes, with or without your racing shoes. You need to find your shoes and either put them on in the house or in the car. If you cannot find your shoes, then you will wear your good shoes all day at school."

"But I don't like my good shoes. They are slow. I like my racing shoes," Andy responded.

"Then you had better find them now," his mother replied.

Andy rushed here and there, searching. Within the two-minute time frame, he had found one in the garage, but could not find the other.

What happened? Andy's mom stuck to her decision. "You are responsible for your racing shoes," she stated. "If you want to wear them to school so that you can run fast, then you will need to keep them in a place where you can find them. If you can't find them, then you will need to wear your good shoes. Do you understand?"

Andy nodded. But he wasn't too happy about wearing "slow" shoes all day.

Fortunately for Andy, there were no important races that day at preschool. After arriving home, he and his mother formed a search committee to find the other shoe, which they did—inside a robot.

"Where do you think you should keep your shoes so that you can find them in the morning?" his mother asked.

Andy thought, then answered, "By my bed. Or maybe in the closet!"

"Good thinking, Andy," his mother chortled. From then on, there were very few mornings that Andy did not have his racing shoes on when it was time to leave.

This SOCCC story can be outlined like this:

Situation	Andy was negligent about finding and putting on his "racing shoes."
Options	He had the option of finding his shoes and putting them on, or wearing his good shoes to school, which he hated.
Choice	Andy was given a limited choice within a timed framework. He needed to find the missing shoes, or wear a less favorite pair to school.
Consequences	He could not find both shoes, so he had to wear his good shoes all day at school.
Consistency	Once Andy's mother settled on an appropriate consequence, she was able to say what she meant, and mean what she said. The victory in this story was the mother's self-control. Faced with her ongoing emo-

tional frustration with Andy, in combination with a time problem, she was extraordinary in her use of self-control.

Taking time to be silent and thinking through the consequences for you as well as for your child *before lashing out* will save much bitterness and grief for both of you.

In our world today, there is so much anger and fear. As long as people believe they have no control over their emotions, these destructive emotions will go unchecked, resulting in destroyed relationships, years of hurt, crime, terrorism, and even war. But if enough children can learn to control their emotions, there is hope for making logical choices and improving our world!

Emotional storms can be calmed by wise decisions following the SOCCC procedure.

INTELLECTUAL CHOICES

Dilemma #1

At three, most children can readily be taught the basics of intellectual functioning. They have a sense of freedom along with a natural curiosity and openness that are refreshing. Helping children to choose to learn and guiding them in the process of that learning is both a joy and a challenge to parents. Intellectual choices eventually determine what people believe about themselves, others, the world, and even God.

Although we definitely don't believe Threes should learn to read, do math, and have homework, we do believe that children can learn to concentrate, develop some attention span, and enjoy learning with an adult. If parents spent more time helping preschoolers learn about things that naturally interest them, would there be less attention-deficit disorders? We don't know, but it is a worthwhile working theory.

Situation   Thelma is the busy mother of two preschoolers. She works at an office all day and has the usual loads of laundry, dirty dishes, and cooking to tackle in the evenings. Her husband teaches school and has papers to grade and lesson plans to formulate.

Billy is three and a half. He is full of energy, wanting to take apart everything he can pry open. It's difficult to get him to sit still long enough to hear about Peter Rabbit or even the exciting adventures of Peter Pan and Wendy.

Mother and Dad are so busy they find themselves going about their own duties, failing to devote their energies to getting Billy to sit still and find fun in stories.

Options

These parents can allow Billy to maintain his high-energy activities and hope that once he gets to kindergarten he'll learn to sit still.

Or, they can become angry or irritated with Billy and try to make him sit and follow a story with them. (Of course, they would probably be unaware that their irritation makes Billy more restless and less able to sit and listen.)

Or they can take turns reading to him for only five minutes at a time. They can show their own enthusiasm about the animals and cars, teaching Billy some of the sounds they make and enjoying his efforts to mimic them.

Choice

Unless these parents are very mature and wise, they may react to Billy according to their own feelings and the stress in their lives. But if they choose the last option above, we believe they'll like it. There's one catch, however—they will have to choose to restrict their personal duties and give top priority to the children's needs.

Consequences

The choice (even by default) to act irritably or to leave Billy to his own devices will result in his being nervous, hyperactive, and feeling rejected or disapproved. His choice will eventually be to rebel or withdraw.

But if Billy's parents take the time, they will be rewarded with a more patient, happy, and well-rounded child.

Consistency

Positive actions, however difficult they may be, will result in a secure and loving bond with Billy that will motivate him to give up some of his energy expenditure in order to feel the closeness with interested and loving parents.

Dilemma #2

The intellectual development of four-year-olds is mushrooming and demands plenty of time and energy. Their "How?" "Why?" and "How come?" questions are infinite.

"How come our cat has only three kittens and Jimmy's had seven?" "What are the stars?" Many of their queries focus on spiritual beliefs. "If Grandpa went to heaven, why was he in that box?"

How can we parents respond to this barrage of questions?

Situation

There are endless questions for which satisfying answers can hardly be found! As a parent, you want so much to find the answers, but no encyclopedia can contain them all. Furthermore, you want to earn your children's respect. You wonder, *If too many interrogations go unanswered, how will the child feel?*

Options

There are many options for you to choose from. You can belittle the child for asking so many "stupid" questions. You could search helplessly for absolutely accurate answers, leaving yourself—and your children—frustrated.

Or you can wisely take time out and sit down with your child. You can ask his own opinion and let him express his suppositions with seriousness. You see, at four, precise answers do not matter a lot. What really matters is the time you take to look into your child's eyes so that he can see respect there and know that he is being taken seriously. If you don't have even an imaginary answer, it's quite a good option to say, "I don't know. You have stumped me! But someday, perhaps one or both of us can find out!"

Choice

In this case, the choice is yours. It includes giving priority time to your child for conversation and attention to his expanding universe. Never again will he or she be quite so curious, open, and trusting. What you teach now will indeed exert a lifelong influence on your child.

Consequences

If you choose wisely, the result will be a giant step toward confidence and security in your child's personality.

Consistency

If you can't find a way to relate comfortably to your four-year-old's questions, it is likely that your child will become more and more distant and less likely to come to you with questions and needs. On the other hand, consistent interaction will reap positive benefits, especially during the turbulent teen years.

The choices of parents and children are so closely intertwined that reactions to each other's wise choices forge the character of every developing child. Be sure that your own intellectual life is rich and full so that it will spill into the waiting sponge of your child's mind. Then both you and your child will be surprised by the wonderful things that happen!

SPIRITUAL CHOICES

Dilemma #1

Our world has been characterized as materialistic, mechanical, pagan, or barbaric. We can bemoan the deterioration around us in helplessness; or we can do something about it. We strongly recommend that you focus on your own spiritual beliefs and the choices that determine these. Then teach these to your children. Spirituality is a sensitive and highly personal area of life, so we recommend a careful approach as in this situation:

Situation   At three years old, Candy does not want to take part in bed-time prayers, but to her parents, this is a vital part of family life.

Options   Candy's parents are worried about her spiritual welfare. They could insist that she say her prayers. They could even spank her for what seems like rebellion.

On the other hand, they could ignore her refusal, blithely believing that someday she will want to join in family prayers.

Or they could realize that God is truly awesome to preschoolers. Candy literally becomes tongue-tied when it comes to praying to a mysterious Being whom she cannot touch, see, or comprehend. Their best option is to teach her slowly about God's characteristics through nature, Bible stories, and their own experiences of him.

Choice

This vital choice demands careful thinking and a prayerful search for divine guidance. Rather than risking a shove toward rebellion by a severe approach, a lot of patience and gentle, occasional encouragement seem wise to us.

Consequences

Giving a child a choice to pray silently or to repeat a brief simple prayer with a parent may result in slow, healthy spiritual growth. Acting worried or becoming angry can be a tragic turnoff to any child's spiritual growth.

Consistency

Parents who consistently lead their children into a knowledge of God by living their lives as examples will be rewarded with questions like, "Mommy, who is

God?" Children will not be afraid to ask questions or search for answers.

Dilemma #2

Four-year-old Tommy was throwing a fit again. As his parents dragged him by the belt into Sunday-school class for the third time in a row, they looked around wildly.

This is so embarrassing! they thought.

Every week it was the same story. Tommy didn't seem at all interested in Sunday school. What should they do with him?

Let's take a look.

Situation	Tommy refuses to go to Sunday-school class. He's throwing a fit in the church hallway.
Options	Tommy's parents have several options.

They could continue to drag him into class and physically force him to sit down in the chair. (But then what will they do for the rest of the class period? And what about the poor teacher who is already looking at them cross-eyed?)

They could take him home and send him, kicking and screaming, to his room and force him to listen to Bible stories.

Or, they could take him to an empty room at the church, sit down with him, and share with him why they want him to be in Sunday school—that it is an important part of their life as a family. They love him and want him to be part of God's family with them.

Choice

Tommy's parents realize that the first choice would be impossible—they (and everyone else around them) would have to listen to Tommy scream for a long time.

And taking him home wouldn't solve anything. They would just have to go through it again next week.

Tommy's parents decide that the third option is best. So they take him to a private room and tell him how important knowing about Jesus is and why they want him to know Jesus too.

Consequences

In the time it takes to find a private room, Tommy's anger diffuses somewhat. He is ready to listen. After his parents explain how important Sunday school is, his defiant "No!"s soften. Even at the age of four, he knows his parents care about him, not just about some silly old Sunday-school class.

Consistency

Because Tommy's parents are consistent in their spiritual home life (they read the Bible together as a family and pray together), Tommy knows that Jesus is important to his parents. He is growing up with a respect and awe for God and a hunger to know and learn more about him.

The spiritual choices you make are the most important ones you will ever make because they concern not only this present life on earth, but your future life. As you learn how to choose wisely for your child, you will enable her to take giant steps toward God and to make good spiritual choices all throughout life!

– 12 –
Older Children
(Ages 5–12)

The ages of five to twelve are vital decision-making years. At around seven or eight, children form their concepts of the world in which they live, and this concept stays with them for life. Of course, they may view their world as a reasonably pleasant and safe one. But all too often, with their limited abilities and poor tools for coping, children become adults who have warped views of themselves as well as their environment. By applying the SOCCC concept, you can prevent your child from making a negative assessment of the world.

In order to understand these elementary-school-age children, it helps to know the basic qualities they need to develop:

1. The foremost lesson for children ages five through twelve is *responsibility*. The foundation of responsibility can be laid even before school if the child has had earlier positive experiences with consistent authority.

2. Next, children must learn the *academic basics*. Mastering skills in reading, writing, and arithmetic is essential for a child's healthy self-esteem. Remember, though, that the process of learning these basics is as important as the end product.

3. Another extremely useful skill is *learning teamwork*. Cooperating at work and play can enhance learning and certainly improves a child's social life.

4. *Healthy competition* is the next lesson for children to learn. We must teach our children that competition can be deadly—a compelling urge to win at all cost. Healthy competition, however, can be a positive motivator to excellence in achievement.

5. *Respect* is a quality many educators believe is rare among children. To learn respect, a child must be respected by both parents and teachers. In order to teach respect, you must take time to listen and teach in a loving, clear, and firm manner. Avoid name-calling, labeling, and any put-downs, and give your child all the compliments he or she can honestly earn. Show respect for your child's friends and siblings as well as for each other as moms and dads.

6. *Self-control* is another quality your child must build into her character. The best minds and keenest insight are useless unless your child has the force of will to follow through with the responsibilities she needs to master.

Now let's explore a few examples of how to help your grade-school children acquire these essential qualities.

RESPONSIBILITY

Dilemma #1

Lisa was nine years old. In her neighborhood, there were no children her age, so she spent time with two older girls, ages thirteen and fourteen.

On this Saturday morning, the girls invited Lisa to go to the mall with them, and since they had no way to get there, they asked if her mother would drive. Lisa's mother agreed. Each girl came to the car with a large shopping bag, saying there were birthday presents to exchange. Lisa's mom arranged to pick them up after they had lunch and exchanged the gifts.

The older girls wanted to eat as soon as they arrived, but since they had no money, they asked Lisa how much she had. She told them, they took it, and they used her money to feed all three of them.

At lunch, Lisa asked what gifts they were exchanging, and what they were going to get. The girls gave vague answers, so Lisa dropped the subject. After all, it seemed reasonable that the big girls wouldn't tell her everything. She was just proud to be in their company.

After lunch, it was time to "shop 'til you drop." Lisa loved to go to the mall, see all the beautiful things, and imagine what she would buy if she could. Since the girls had taken all her money, she had none for spending. But that was O.K. Today she would look. After all, it was fun to be with teenagers. And this was the first time they had ever invited her to the mall.

The girls went into several different stores, looking at things, but not exchanging the birthday gifts. In fact, when Lisa peeked in one of the bags, she didn't see anything. *Oh well,* she thought. *Maybe they just brought a really big bag for a small gift, hoping to get something bigger and better.*

Then Lisa took another look, and gasped. There were a lot of things in both bags, and none of them were in store wrappings. "What are you doing?" she asked the girls.

"Shut-up, Lisa. What do you think we're doing? We're shopping!" the girls said sarcastically.

"But you don't have any money!" Lisa retorted.

"Oh really, little girl? So what? We've learned to shop without money, stupid!" one of the girls snarled. "And now, cuz you're such a *nice* little girl, we'll teach you," the other girl taunted.

"Th-that's O.K.," Lisa whispered. "You d-d-don-t have to. I do-don-t mind not-t- g-g-getting anything."

"But we *want* you to have something," one of the girls said persuasively. "See that jewelry over there?" Lisa barely nodded. "Take this bag, go over to where the pins and earring are, and just slide something into the bag."

"B-but I really don't w-w-want to," Lisa said.

"Do you want to be our friend?" one of the girls asked vehemently.

"Yes," Lisa replied.

"Then do what I say, or we can't be friends with you!"

The other girl chimed in, "That's right! Take the bag, and get a piece of jewelry in it, or we'll never speak to you again!"

Lisa was scared. She knew that stealing was wrong, but she really liked the older girls a lot. After all, they were her friends, and had even asked her to go to the mall with them. She didn't want to do what was wrong, but she wanted them to be her friends. She needed to be sure. "If I do what you say, you'll be my friends?"

"Right," the girls said. "But you'd better do it right now, or we won't!"

They shoved the bag into Lisa's hand and gave her a nudge toward the jewelry counter. Lisa was very nervous as she edged toward the counter, then looked back. "Go on," the girls mouthed, smiling.

Lisa was at the counter, looking around. The salesgirl had her back turned; she was busy helping someone else. Jittery fingers reached out and slid a pin from the counter. The pin slipped onto the floor. Lisa became more scared. She looked at the girls. They had their backs turned and were in another part of the store. Quickly Lisa picked up the pin, threw it in the bag, and went to meet her friends.

"Did you do it?" they asked. Lisa smiled weakly. "Let's see." She opened the bag. The pin lay on top. "Cool! That wasn't so hard, was it?" Lisa wasn't so sure. "The more you do it, the more fun it is," laughed one girl. "Right?" The other girl giggled in aggreement.

They left the store. In a matter of moments, the mall police came up and escorted the girls into an office. Lisa was horrified. Now the other girls looked scared, too. The police dumped both bags onto a large table. Out came sweaters, jewelry, cosmetics, and a handbag. The police asked many questions, then called the parents.

Lisa's mother arrived first. By this time, Lisa was sobbing with regret and fear. The other girls were silent. The police were serious.

Stunned at hearing the tale, Lisa's mother asked the police what would happen to her daughter. Because of her age, and because it was a first offense, she could take her daughter home. Both Lisa and her mother assured the police it would never happen again.

The other girls were asked to remain until their parents came, and a decision concerning them would be made.

At first dumbfounded, Lisa's mother comforted her daughter, assured her of her love and forgiveness, and began to talk gently to her about the meaning of true friendship. Lisa learned a lesson she has not forgotten. In the years that have followed, with careful guidance from her mother, she has chosen friends more wisely, and has never been involved in a similar incident.

Lisa's story can be put into the SOCCC framework:

Situation   Lisa was at the mall with two teenagers who were stealing and wanted Lisa to steal.

Options   Lisa could steal to earn the girls' friendship. But she could also get into trouble with the police and her parents. Lisa could choose not to steal and lose the friendship of the older girls.

Choice   Lisa chose to steal.

Consequences The girls were taken for questioning by the mall police, the stolen items were retrieved, and the parents were brought into the situation. Because of the efforts of her mother, Lisa began to learn about friendship and what the consequences of succumbing to peer group pressure really are.

Consistency   Lisa's mother believed these girls were "friends" and could be trusted. She was deceived by them. She also recognized that her daughter succumbed to peer-group pressure and needed her support and guidance. She gave guided support during and following the incident, as both she and Lisa learned to make better decisions.

How fortunate for Lisa that she had a mother who understood the strength of the pressure her daughter experienced and who behaved with controlled reason. Had the mother flown off the handle, screaming such things as, "How could you do this to your father and me? This has never happened in our family before! Why would you steal something you don't even want, when your father and I provide everything you need?", she would have humiliated her daughter further and caused Lisa to withdraw into quiet anger at a time when she desperately needed loving support and guidance, not harsh criticism. Seeds of rebellion could have been planted in Lisa that could have thrown her into alliances with other "friends" who would have led her further astray through the years.

Instead, Lisa now realizes that she must choose to do right even when "friends" are doing wrong.

ACADEMIC ACHIEVEMENT

Dilemma #1

In today's extremely technical world, acquiring knowledge can open many options for young people's futures. But, at the immediate moment, many children don't enjoy studying. Why? Studying requires postponing pleasure now in the interest of future good.

How will your child choose to learn? Here is an example that we hope will help.

Situation   Eric consistently convinced his parents that he had no homework. They were glad he could enjoy the bike neither of them had as children. His fun-loving nature was a joy to live with. But Eric's mid-semester grades were failing. The school staff were concerned and arranged a conference to help Eric and his parents.

Options   Eric's parents could allow him to fail and hope he would do better later.

They could punish and ground him, risking total rebellion and even more failure.

Or they could find a means of motivating Eric.

Choice   First, Eric's mother made her choice and established a well-defined plan. One day when Eric came home from school, Mother was settled into an easy chair reading the evening paper. At first she ignored him, but finally she stated matter-of-factly, "Eric, I just want to enjoy my paper this evening. There will be no dinner until you finish your homework and straighten your room, too." Mother resumed reading.

Eric was stunned into silence. At long last he pleaded, "No dinner, Mama?"

Mother casually replied, "That's right, Eric. You heard me! No dinner. To me, responsible study habits seem as important as food." Again, she read.

When he saw that her actions and words were identical and realized she meant business, Eric set to work. His room was orderly in a short time and the homework done neatly.

Mother realized that at last Eric knew she meant business and was not going to stop with just yelling. She had taught him to make a wise choice.

Consequences Short-term results were gratifying to both mother and son. His room was clean, and he could attend school prepared for classes. Mother felt successful and pleased that she had helped Eric learn some basic responsibility. The long-term consequence, of course, depended on Mother's follow-through.

Consistency If Mother practices the third big "C" (consistency) long enough, Eric will certainly learn good habits of reliability and excellent values, as well as the thrill of regular success.

TEAMWORK

Dilemma #1

Marie was a happy child who enjoyed play, reading, and imagining all sorts of exotic adventures. She also had several appropriate jobs to do each evening at home. But often her mind and heart were so busy that she forgot to complete those jobs.

What should her parents do?

Situation   Marie forgot to prepare the food necessary to make several school lunches the next morning. This was one of her jobs as part of the family team. She had forgotten the task several times in the past weeks, and her mother had patiently fulfilled Marie's duties for her.

Options   The options were really for her parents! They loved Marie's joyful nature and, after all, it was not a hard task for Mom to do.

They could continue to do Marie's job for her.

A second option was to let the task wait until morning, hoping there would be time to complete it then.

But Dad thought of a third possibility—to awaken Marie and have her do that job, late as it was, emphasizing the fact that Mom was busy handling her portions of the family work and that the family members were depending on Marie to handle hers.

Choice

The parents chose the latter course. Father sternly called Marie from a sound sleep and silently guided her to the area of her neglected responsibility. He stood by while she sheepishly, belatedly did the work. Then, with a twinkle in his brown eyes, he humorously tweaked her ear and sent her back to bed.

Consequences

Marie's sensitive soul was not offended by her father's discipline, and she learned to do her jobs at the proper time. Never again did she need to get out of bed to fulfill her responsibility.

Consistency

Because Marie's parents were consistent in making sure that she accomplished her tasks, she learned to choose to be responsible.

HEALTHY COMPETITION

Dilemma #1

The pendulum of values swings widely in our Western culture. Only a few years ago, many people advocated curtailing competition among children. They felt that by its very definition, rivalry meant that some had to lose so others could win. Another point of view, however, is that competition is a fact of life, and it must be understood and regulated to keep it from becoming "deadly."

How can you use the SOCCC approach to teach motivating, fun competition to your children?

Situation   Randy was slender and lithe, well-coordinated, and full of energy—a good candidate for gymnastics. He had always insisted on winning at games and this push for success further enhanced his potential to become a good gymnast.

Options   Besides gymnastics, Randy was also in-
                   terested in baseball, music, and scouts.
                   He was a solid student, but he had to
                   study to maintain his grades.

                   His parents wanted Randy to have
                   plenty of opportunities to grow but also
                   wanted to avoid his being over-burdened.

Choice   Randy and his parents sat down
                   together, listed his activities, and dis-
                   cussed the value of competing in a new
                   field. One of the values of gymnastics is
                   the opportunity to compete against your-
                   self as well as others. Being able to lose
                   in a sportsmanlike manner and to win
                   graciously would be good qualities for
                   Randy to develop.

                   Together Randy and his mom and dad
                   chose to give up baseball and his clarinet
                   lessons so he could explore this new op-
                   portunity.

Consequences   Randy learned some good techniques for
                   making decisions—honestly assessing
                   how much time and energy he had and
                   how to determine priorities. Further-
                   more, Randy embarked on a long journey
                   that would teach him the value of healthy
                   competition.

Consistency   Because Randy and his parents had had
                   consistent times together as a family in

both work and play, they could sit down and determine their priorities and what they could learn together.

Whether it is in playing games at home, participating in community sports teams, or entering various competitions in school, children can learn a great deal from pitting their skills against others. Help your child learn how to win, how to lose(!) and how to be the best he or she can be!

RESPECT

Dilemma #1

This quality, so sadly lacking in today's world, must be carefully taught. It doesn't happen automatically. You may not have realized how much respect is related to the ability to make good choices. In fact, you may have thought it had to be drilled into your children.

Let's consider how choices work.

Situation

For the "umpteenth" time, Tony, a third-grader, has failed to empty the overflowing trash-basket. Mother has reminded him and told him how lazy and irresponsible he is. She has let him know that when he grows up he will have a hard time of it—if he makes it at all. Lately she has been yelling at him constantly (in her understandable frustration).

In spite of this, Tony loves his mom. He knows that in most of her life she is kind and fun-loving. But that doesn't make it any easier for him.

When there is a problem at school, or a sports activity doesn't work out well, or classmates fail to act as he wishes they would, Tony acts out his frustration. He yells at both his teacher and his peers. Many of the angry things he'd like to retort to his mother, he spills onto others.

Options

As always, options are arranged along a spectrum. Mother has more options than she has realized for dealing with Tony's forgetfulness.

First of all, she can develop and practice an attitude of unswerving respect for Tony. In choosing this option, she need not lose her needed parental position. She can then focus on the option of making an important privilege contingent upon his becoming responsible. She can reduce his allowance. She can even enlist Tony's help in setting up a plan that will teach him to be responsible.

The sad option, of course, remains. She can continue to scream and put down her own son, furthering the poor example!

Choice

Tony's problems at school could jolt both mother and son out of their painful rut. If he becomes bad enough, the school staff will probably seek her help for Tony, and, just maybe, she will see her own pattern of negative reacting more clearly. The teacher, however, can help Tony choose better responses. We know one school principal who has any misbehaving child come and visit with him. He makes certain the child understands his error and then has him write out a corrective plan. Both he and the teacher then work with that child to effect the changes the child has chosen.

Consequences   This principal's method seems to work well. It helps children think clearly and honestly, use their own mental ability to choose wisely, and yet provides adult support that is positive and truly corrective. If Tony refuses to cooperate, of course, and if Mom fails to see how important her input is, the ultimate negative result can be the growing disrespect that could cause Tony to become violent at some point.

Consistency   Tony's mom must learn to be loving and consistent in her actions and speech toward her son. If she works hard in this area, she's bound to see wonderful paybacks for the time and energy she invests.

Children in grade school are so teachable. As a parent, you are privileged to teach them the power of choosing right attitudes, behaviors, and character ingredients that will make their lives a success.

SELF-CONTROL

Dilemma #1

Sometime in the 1980's, Americans reacted against the "let-it-all-hang-out" philosophy of the prior decade. Aha! So there *is* a semblance of self-control in society! Under the "dress for success" superficiality, however, there lurks a great deal of angry impulsiveness. For example, though career women have learned to avoid tears because tears seem weak, they sometimes still scream out their frustrations at home and find effective (even cruel) means of getting even. So do men!

Lack of emotional control is a serious problem in our modern-day society. In promoting children's rights, it is easy to allow them to express their emotions in ways that embarrass them later on. Schoolmates may withdraw from such poorly controlled children, leaving them lonely but puzzled.

That's what happened to eleven-year-old Peter. Abandoned by his father as a baby, Peter lived with his older brother, who was known for his truancy, and his mother, who worked hard to make a home for the boys in a tiny apartment.

Through generous friends, a scholarship was awarded to Peter that enabled him to attend a private school. His mother was elated and looked forward to the personal attention and love that Peter would receive. He seemed to thrive in the atmosphere, and although he had to work hard to overcome poor study habits, he did passing work, was well-liked by the other students, and excelled in sports.

The following year, he was again awarded a scholarship. During the summer, prior to his entrance in sixth grade, Peter was accused of bullying smaller children several times. The principal talked with him, mentioned his excellent record, and discussed the importance of developing self-control. Peter understood and cooperated, and all was pleasant—for awhile.

Unfortunately, the bullying activity did not stop, and similar conversations took place over a period of months between the principal and Peter. When Peter was sent to the office yet again, the principal reminded him that he was there on a scholarship because the school believed in his potential. He was also told, "Peter, I cannot 'make' you stop bullying and hitting. Really, no one can. It is a choice that you will have to make. If you choose to stop this, you may stay in our school, and we will be glad to have you. However, if you choose to keep up the bullying and hitting, then you will not be able to attend our school and will have to look for another place. It is my choice that you stay in the school. I care for you, so do the teachers, and the other kids like you also, unless you hit or bully them. Peter, do you want to be in this school?" Peter said he did. "Do we treat you with kindness?" Peter felt they did. "You know then that if you are going to stay here, you are going to have to keep your hands to yourself." Peter said he would.

Several days later, a girl with a bloodied face and broken, bleeding places on her legs, arms, and hands was helped into the office. She had passed out face down on the black-top, where she had sustained the injuries. When she was taken to emergency, the doctors discovered that she had a concussion in addition to her surface wounds.

Who had done this? *Peter*. The girl told her story. "Peter asked if I wanted to play a new game called 'Black-out.' I said, 'Sure.' Then he put his hands on my neck, and pressed until I passed out."

The elementary principal and staff were incredulous that this had happened on their campus. Peter came in, looking very sad and guilty. He acknowledged what he had done, had no particular reason for doing it, and was reminded of the school rules and of previous conversations.

"Peter, we had agreed that if this type of behavior continued, it would mean that you had not chosen to use self-control in keeping your hands to yourself. Is that right?"

"I didn't mean to do it. I didn't know she would really black out." Peter hung his head.

"Did you know that the school rules say that you are to keep your hands to yourself?" Peter nodded. "Do you remember our discussions about choices?" Peter acknowledged he did. "Peter, it looks like you have made your choice. You have chosen to defy the rules of our school again and again. I am so sorry. I wanted you to be able to remain in our school, but we cannot have people playing games that cause concussions and injuries. You will need to find another school to attend."

Peter was silent. Several minutes later he began to cry, realizing the consequence of his choice.

Several weeks later, someone asked the principal, "Don't you think Peter has learned his lesson?" The principal hoped he had, for his sake. "Don't you want to ask him back?" The principal shook his head no. "Peter knew the rules, had been warned repeatedly, and had been repeatedly told he was welcome in the school on scholarship for as long as he chose to obey the rules. He made his choice. The entire school witnessed what he did. We have to protect all our children and let them know that our school is a safe place."

Situation	Twelve-year-old old Peter was repeatedly bullying and hitting smaller children on the play yard.
Options	Peter was warned repeatedly about his behavior. He was given the option of exerting self-control and staying in the school or continuing his behavior and finding another school to attend.
Choice	Peter made the choice to continue his behavior and accelerate the activity.
Consequences	He was asked to leave the school, following an incident that resulted in multiple injuries.
Consistency	The principal was consistent. The playground rules had been established for the safety of all. Peter knew them, was warned repeatedly, and was encouraged

to make a choice for self-control. He did
not do this, so the principal followed
through on the consequence. Peter had to
leave the school.

When something like this happens on a school campus,
it demonstrates to the parents and students that the school
leadership can be counted on to uphold safety policies for
the protection of others.

Peter's increased aggression was really a cry for help.
Therapy was strongly recommended long before the final
incident, but Peter's mom postponed counseling indefinite-
ly. Perhaps with a different choice for therapy, the consequence would have been far different for Peter.

Dilemma #2

Self-control can relate to decisions about actions (such as
Peter's decision to bully the other children) or emotions.
Stan had problems choosing how to act emotionally.

Situation   Stan had often watched wide-eyed as his
dad lost control in his workshop. If Dad
had trouble with his saw or failed to
measure accurately, he would swear and
get red in the face. Other times, he was
good-natured and fun to play ball with.

When Stan missed problems in his
sixth-grade math book or struck out playing baseball, he, too, became angry. After
all, he had watched Dad. And isn't that
how Dad handled his anger?

Options   Both Stan and his father are reacting to
                     frustrations with poor self-control. It's
                     understandable to be upset when things
                     go wrong. But to set an example (or to
                     follow it) of taking out such feelings in a
                     two-year-old tantrum fashion is not ac-
                     ceptable. Better options include: slowing
                     down in order to avoid mistakes, seeking
                     help when it's needed, taking time out to
                     calm down, or simply stating (perhaps
                     silently to one's self), "I feel so angry
                     when I make mistakes!"

Choice   It's difficult to change when you have felt
                     temporarily powerful for years during
                     angry outbursts. Choosing to use self-
                     control will not be easy for Dad or Stan.

                     If, however, Dad discovers that his son
                     is demonstrating similar private out-
                     bursts in school, he may decide it's time
                     for both father and son to develop new
                     habits. And when the school counselor
                     solicits Stan's parents' help for his bad
                     blow-ups, Stan, himself, may decide to
                     change.

Consequences   When self-control is applied properly,
                     everyone is likely to function and feel
                     better. If neither Dad nor Stan is willing
                     to make the efforts to change, of course,
                     the old pattern of intimidating others
                     (and later feeling guilty and remorseful)

will continue. They will have to choose whether they want to live with bad feelings and impaired relationships or not.

Consistency   Stan's dad needs to develop new ways of handling his own anger to be able to help his son. He can't teach his son emotional stability unless he himself is consistent in practicing what he preaches.

Dilemma #3

Another difficult area related to poor self-control is indulgence. All of us would rather have fun than work. After all, pleasure is certainly preferable to pain! Children who don't learn to choose properly may always choose the easy avenues, avoiding pain and focusing on fun.

You can see where this path will end. The child who gives up sports when he loses his first game or quits skating when she falls and skins her knee will have a most difficult time finishing school and eventually finding and keeping a job.

Children must learn how to turn negative emotions like disappointment, frustration, even intense anger, into a positive experience. And that's exactly what Allen's mom taught him how to do.

Allen was an emotionally volatile child with strong opinions. While on a Christmas shopping excursion with his mother, he expected her to make unreasonable purchases that far exceeded her budget. When she firmly clarified the amount they could spend, Allen responded with intense anger in a rude and even embarrassing manner.

Situation   It was not the shopping that created the
problem, but Allen's response to reason-
able limit-setting. His behavior was
offensive to both his mother and the by-
standers and certainly could not go un-
challenged. His behavior, however, was
prompted by his disappointment as well
by his habit of manipulating his mom and
others through anger.

Options   Hastily Allen's mother assessed the situation. As she took Allen out to the parking
lot on the way toward the car, she listed
his options whiled he marched along in
angry silence.

- Allen could change his attitude, handle his emotions better, and they could
  return to the store.
- He could change his attitude and they
  would go home to do something fun
  that he could choose.
- They could go home with his anger still
  steaming and have a miserable evening.

Allen had to choose, and they were not
leaving until he did.

Choice   It was a long wait, the hostile silence
broken only by Mother's occasional

words of explanation or encouragement. At last, Allen wrote on a scrap of paper the terse message, "Back in!!!"

Mother was surprised and made certain Allen knew the type of pleasant cooperation that she expected. He was, indeed, able to gain control of his disappointment and his anger.

Consequences   Mother was delighted to see Allen's growth in self-control and his ability to get over those negative feelings and actions. She told him she was proud of his achievement and acknowledged that at his age she had not done so well. Both mother and son had great pleasure as they prepared for Christmas giving. And Allen quietly glowed with pride in his own victory.

Consistency   Allen's mother chose, in love, not to let Allen get away with selfish, uncontrolled behavior. She knew that curbing this behavior would assist him now *and* in the future. So even though standing strong on this issue was more difficult (at the moment) than letting Allen get away with his anger, she chose to be consistent in her discipline—and her method of giving him the responsibility of choices and the following consequences.

Dilemma #4

Learning self-control demands guidance and the reinforcement of right choices in the crucial years of five to twelve. Almost all children want to be popular and successful. When peers are experimenting with exciting and aggressive things (such as sex, alcohol, and drugs), will your child have the self-control to stand alone? Even children with good self-esteem cannot always resist temptation unless they have self-control, too.

It helps to have a firm foundation of self-control, as Marilyn and her parents discovered.

Situation

Marilyn's eyes were glued to the five kids who were huddled together in a corner of the playground. They seemed to be having so much fun. Her very best friend, Sue, was one of them, and Marilyn felt sad because she was shut-out by them.

During her fifth-grade class, Marilyn wrote a note asking Sue what was so much fun. After a while a reply came back, "Denny brought some beer from home, and we were all tasting it. Next time you can have some too, O.K.?"

Options

Marilyn knew that beer was an alcoholic drug. What were her options?

She knew she could go along with the gang and explore the excitement of forbidden experiences.

She could join the group and not drink with them and probably keep her friendship.

She could refuse to join and risk losing her best friend.

Or she could tell her teacher what was going on and hope her friends would all be stopped before they went too far.

Quite a list of possibilities for a nice, ordinary eleven-year-old!

Choice

With doubts in her mind and concern on her face, Marilyn quietly nodded, "O.K.!" Not a good choice, but understandable. The doubts remained, however, and that night Marilyn happened to see an ad on TV that talked about the sadness of alcoholism.

In the morning, Marilyn awoke wondering if today would be the first time she tasted alcohol. She finally faced her doubts squarely. "Why should I take the risk? If Sue is really my friend, she'll like me even if I don't drink beer. And if she's not my friend, why should I drink beer with her?"

Consequences

Because of a variety of influences, Marilyn was able to say "No!" to a big temptation. The positive consequences were the firming up of her good values, self-control, and wise choosing. Her good feelings reinforced her decision, and not having to feel guilty and afraid of being getting caught added to her elation.

Eventually she did lose her friendship with Sue, but, as she said to herself, "Who needs a friend who gets you in trouble?"

Consistency   Marilyn has her parents to thank for getting her out of this bad situation. Ever since she was little, they taught her the value of good choices and talked about peer pressure. They showed her how important it is to be consistent with her values in her everyday actions.

The power to choose is a priceless gift! We hope you are becoming excited about teaching the skills of good decision making to your children and about learning them yourselves!

The Hurried Child

In 1981, Dr. David Elkind wrote a thought-provoking book called *The Hurried Child.*[1] Even then a great many people could see the danger and tragedy of children who grow up too soon. And today it seems the hurrying process is accelerating even more rapidly.

Over the last few years, the middle-school movement has hit the United States. At first middle schools seemed like a great idea. Perhaps seventh and eighth graders could stay children just a bit longer. They could be assigned special teachers with whom they could relate as a mentor. And the heroic efforts of parents to teach responsibility and other healthy values would be reinforced by the school staff. Perhaps, in fact, the damaging process of hurrying our children could be slowed down.

Unfortunately, this rarely happens. Instead, the push to grow up quickly has now invaded children in the sixth grade. There are increasing influences pushing pre- or early-adolescent youngsters to hurry and grow up. Classes are rotated every hour so that children must adjust often to different teacher personalities. Rarely do our children have time just to look out of the windows and relish the blue sky, white clouds, or a passing blackbird.

What Pre-Adolescents Need from You

Today the choices and options facing our pre-adolescents are overwhelming. Many of them have excessive freedom without rules or supervision. Concurrently, they are exposed to sexual stimulation they can feel but not really comprehend—much less control. The availability of drugs and alcohol is amazingly easy. Shopping malls as well as school hallways are ready-made markets for students and professional dealers to make quick money. Eager, curious, and often lonely kids are easy prey for these mercenary sharks. If ever children need to know how to make wise choices, they need to know before and during pre-adolescence.

Parents must assume *more* responsibility in these crucial years, not less! In spite of your children's pseudo-sophistication, do not be misled. You cannot, of course, put them back in the safety of the play pen (much as you'd like to at times). But you *can* do some specific things to help.

- You can become just a bit more of a friend to your child, not quite so much parent. The balance is important.

- You still must create, adjust, and maintain proper bottom lines. Certainly your child needs a bit more freedom and slightly less supervision, but she must have even more careful surveillance from a little greater distance. Your child must be pulled in before she reaches disaster zones.

- This is the time to remember the past—your child's and your own—and share it. Stories about special, tender, and funny events bear re-telling. Bedtime (when we all are somewhat vulnerable and open) is a good time to share stories. Stories that will reveal your own feelings and struggles during this period of your life will help your child feel understood—no matter what she's going through. Always include some aspect that will remind your child of the power of choice.

- Welcome your child's friends and carefully guide your son or daughter to choose close friendships that are positive.

- Practice all the skills you can find that will teach your pre-adolescent to choose wisely.

Keeping this list in mind will encourage you through the ups and downs of parenting and will bring to mind good times together—for both you and your child.

Reminders for Parents

You have been given a great responsibility, but not an impossible one. Here are some suggestions that can help you deal with your own emotions and encourage you to be consistent in words and in action.

- Avoid emotional decisions that usually include power-struggles.

- Gather all the important information about the decision your child faces—on all sides of the issue.

- From this information, clarify the options. What are all the possible choices available—good or bad?

- Use logic and will to make good decisions—not wishes and emotions. Help your child use self-control.

- Make clear the consequences of any given choice. "If you choose X, what will the results be?"

- Carefully avoid an "I told you so, Stupid!" attitude.

- Be consistent day by day, season after season. The effort of being consistent reaps great rewards in the lives of children.

Some extra time and energy during these important months of your child's pre-adolescence can complete a strong foundation for your child's next wise choices! No effort you put into your child's emotional, spiritual, physical, and intellectual growth will ever be wasted.

– 13 –
Adolescents and Young Adults
(Ages 12–20)

Choices during this period certainly are not child's play. They may in fact, become deadly serious. Suicide, depression, social problems, sexual looseness, and even crime are regular headlines in the media. Developmentally, the biggest task any adolescent faces is that of finishing the growing-up process.

Becoming independent in a non-rebellious manner is the assignment that creates so much conflict and confusion in families who have adolescents and young adults. But if you have taught your children how to choose wisely in the small issues of life, you will have prepared them well for the major decisions they face from twelve to twenty.

What are some of the major decisions that your adolescent or young adult will face? These are just a few:

- What kind of attitude will I have toward life in general?

- How will I manage my money?

- How do I control myself when faced with peer pressure?

- In what areas must I be responsible?

- What will I do for my life's work?

No wonder your adolescent or young adult feels she is on a roller-coaster ride! She is weighted with the heavy responsibility of big choices.

Let's take a look at some of these major decisions from the SOCCC approach.

ATTITUDES

Dilemma #1

Day by day, Nancy, an eighth grader, became more moody and distant. She no longer studied at all, and her grades had zoomed from near the top of her class to mostly failing ones. She was moody, rude, and found only a few friends who would tolerate her careless dress and poor hygiene.

Nancy said she didn't care about life at all, because life was a chore anyway. She was a prime example of a *bad attitude*.

Situation   Nancy told her counselor, after many weeks of deterioration, that she was smoking marijuana, drinking, and occasionally taking stronger drugs.

Looking back at a lost school year, her counselor asked, "Nancy, what could we have done to help you sooner? What would have stopped your trouble?"

Nancy pondered before answering, "Before junior high, I never did anything wrong. I was a perfect child because Mom and Dad bossed my whole life. So when I started sneaking out of the house at night, they never guessed. I think if even one person had noticed what I was doing and had tried to stop me, I would have changed."

Options

Nancy and her parents both, of course, had more options than they realized. Their old habits had been limiting. The parents had always made the decisions, and their relationship with Nancy was strong enough that she had always obeyed. But when faced with a situation in which she could finally choose for herself, Nancy had no experience that could help her make good decisions. Had she known how to list the options, Nancy would have seen that she could get help from her teachers, counselor, and yes—even from her parents and grandmother. She might have dressed more appropriately, done her homework, and refused drugs.

Choice

Nancy's parents had not chosen well, early on, the way they would rear Nancy. Nancy chose extremely poorly until finally she was so frightened that she tried to take her life—she made a silent plea for help by swallowing a bottle of pain relievers.

Consequences

The results could have been disastrous. Nancy actually tried to take her life (as many other teens do each year). But she really didn't want to die, so she made sure her parents would be home and then called a friend who, fortunately, notified her parents.

At last Nancy got the help she'd been looking for, and she worked well with the counselor her parents found. With good professional help and the new options the whole family learned, Nancy's consequences were positive.

Consistency   Unfortunately, Nancy's parents were consistent in one thing—choosing poorly. Instead of allowing Nancy room to grow and explore, they made all decisions for her. Then when Nancy experienced some of "the real world," she was extremely frightened.

Dilemma #2

Nicole was not a good student, but was capable of earning passing grades. What bothered her parents more than her poor grades, however, were the "U"s (Unsatisfactory) in cooperation. They firmly believed that their daughter could get an "S" (Satisfactory) in cooperation and that a "U" was a reflection of an unacceptable attitude.

At the beginning of her junior year, they told her that each "U" on her report card would cost her $50.00 in babysitting, payable at her usual babysitting rate per hour. There were two very young children in her family, so there was always plenty of babysitting available for Nicole.

Nicole had agreed to try to improve. But she was *positive* that some of the teachers didn't like her, and she certainly didn't like them. Her parents' advice? "Do your best and keep your mouth shut!"

When Nicole was sixteen, she enrolled in a Driver's Education class. Within a short time, she was convinced that the teacher "did not like women," and so, of course, he did not like her. Therefore, Nicole didn't like him—and she made that feeling very obvious to the teacher.

Her parents responded with disappointment and a warning. "Nicole, whether the teacher likes you or not is immaterial. There will be many people along the way in life that may not like you, and you will need to learn to get along with them. Please do it now with this teacher. Keep yourself under control, don't say what comes to your mind, get an 'S,' and save yourself a lot of unpaid work."

One Sunday evening at 9:00, Nicole remembered that she was supposed to outline a chapter for the class. She moaned and groaned about it, asking her parents, "Do I have to do it?"

"Absolutely not," they replied. "It is your choice whether you ever do any work for the class or not. If you want to pass, you should do the work. If you don't care and you want to repeat the class in summer school instead of going to basketball camp and being on the team next year, then don't outline this chapter or any other chapter."

Because it was late and she didn't feel like doing it, Nicole chose not to outline the chapter (although she loved basketball camp and wanted to be on the team).

There were various tests throughout the course. Again, Nicole made a choice. "I don't need to study this stuff. I already know enough."

Again her parents responded, "It's up to you, Nicole. You know the consequences of both an 'Unsatisfactory' and a failure to pass the course."

What happened to Nicole? Well, she got an "F" (Failure) in her Driver's Ed course. In addition, she was given a "U" (Unsatisfactory) in cooperation, with a note from the teacher indicating that it was due to her ongoing sarcastic attitude.

Nicole screamed, "Unfair! I don't deserve an 'F.' I should get at least a 'D'—."

Her parents suggested, "If you feel it is unfair, then you need to make an appointment to see the instructor and discuss it with him."

At first, Nicole determined to do just that. But after considering her test results and the several homework assignments she chose to ignore, Nicole thought it best to leave things as they were.

The consequences came. In addition to the $50.00 worth of babysitting, Nicole did not qualify to go to basketball camp in the summer, and because of her "F," she was not eligible to try out for the team. She spent the summer babysitting and repeating driver's education . . . with the same teacher!

Nicole's story is unfortunate.

Situation   Nicole needed to pass Driver's Ed to be eligible for the basketball team and to attend basketball camp. She also needed to avoid getting a "U" in cooperation, or she would do a considerable number of free hours of babysitting.

Options   Nicole had the option of exerting self-control and getting a "Satisfactory" or mouthing-off and getting a "U." She also had the option of studying and doing homework assignments and passing the class or failing the class, taking it over in summer school, and missing the opportunity of being on the basketball team and attending basketball camp.

Choice

Nicole made the choice to mouth off to the instructor and not to study.

Consequences

Nicole received an "Unsatisfactory" in cooperation, and had to work off $50.00 worth of free babysitting. Because of her "F" in the class, she was ineligible for the basketball team, had to retake the class in summer school, and was unable to attend basketball camp.

Consistency

Nicole's parents were consistent in their commitment to let Nicole choose and accept the responsibility for the consequences of her choices. They did not rescue or scream.

As a parent, you can choose the pattern of consistency and teach your children good decision-making skills. You can choose to act positively about life and its ups and downs. If you do these things, you are giving valuable gifts to your children.

MONEY MANAGEMENT

Dilemma #1

Fourteen-year-old Valerie loved clothes and was particularly attracted to designer labels. Any article of clothing—jeans, belts, handbags, tops, or undergarments—was that much better *if* the designer label was in plain view.

Her parents did not object to their daughter being well dressed, but they were somewhat aghast at the prices of the merchandise she preferred. Each year the prices escalated along with Valerie's "needs." Something had to be done. Valerie's parents had a private talk about the problem and came up with what appeared to be a reasonable solution.

Throughout the years, Valerie's dad had made it a habit to take his daughter out for dinner from time to time, a special "Dad 'n Daughter evening" that they both looked forward to and enjoyed. On this particular evening, Valerie's dad presented the idea of a clothing allowance to her. He would give Valerie a certain amount of money in August so that she could purchase whatever she "needed" for the new school year, but this money had to pay for all wearables, including such items as jewelry and shoes. Her dad explained that he wanted her to have the freedom to spend the money in whatever way she desired and the responsibility for using the money wisely.

Valerie loved the idea, so she and her dad discussed financial details that were fair to both. Her dad warned her about extravagance and what that would mean, emphasizing that she would not be given any money for clothing by either parent until the next installment in January. Valerie listened carefully, agreed to all stipulations, and the deal was done!

An ecstatic Valerie went shopping. At first the money seemed like a lot, but soon she realized that it wasn't enough for her taste. She knew her parents meant what they said, and that there was no way she was getting any more money. She had to make a list of priority items and select carefully. She had to decide whether it was more important to have the designer jeans or an extra pair of boots. She had to make other decisions that slowed down the shopping expedition.

That afternoon she came home with fewer outfits than she had anticipated, but with a greater understanding of just how far money can go and why her parents wanted her to have control of the spending.

"You guys were just hopin' I'd find out about the value of money, weren't you?" Her parents laughed and asked how the experiment was going. "Well, as you know," Valerie commented, "I absolutely LOVE designer stuff, but I figured out I will have to survive without some things I really thought I had to have. But I did get the really, really important things that I'll wear the most and that show the most. Do you get it?"

"Oh, we get it!" Valerie's parents realized that this experiment was giving their daughter responsibility for the money as well as money-management lessons that would benefit her for the rest of her life. They also noticed that Valerie's confidence and self-assurance grew as a result of the fiscal responsibility. They have continued this practice with great success.

Situation	Valerie had extravagant taste in clothes, so her parents decided to give her a clothing allowance.
Options	Valerie had the opportunity to purchase as much or as little as she could with the money, knowing the money would not be supplemented in any way by her parents until the next installment several months away.
Choice	After discovering that the money she had was not enough for all she wanted, Valerie prioritized. She made a list, making certain she bought the clothes that were most important to her.
Consequences	Valerie's confidence and self-assurance grew as a result of the fiscal responsibility.
Consistency	Valerie's SOCCC parents were consistent in their child rearing, so she knew they meant what they said, *the first time*. She

operated with security within the agreed financial boundaries.

If parents who have rescued their child from consequences in the past were to try this, it is almost inevitable that the daughter would test the boundaries to see if the parent really meant what was said, or if there was a way to get more money by whining and pleading. It is imperative that both parent and child initially agree on the financial terms and that they abide by these terms.

SELF-CONTROL

Dilemma #1

Janelle was nearly eighteen—a young woman of immense energy and boundless curiosity. Her grades were high, and she was very involved in extra-curricular activities. She was a star basketball player, and while she hated the team rules, she knew the policies helped keep her life under control.

All was not going well at Janelle's home. On top of all her school pressures and busy lifestyle, she was worried about her parents' marriage and confused about her role in trying to mend it. She felt pulled in several directions at once.

Situation   Janelle, now a senior in high school, began to spend extended hours with a boyfriend and was debating whether or not to give in to his sexual advances. She received from him the love and attention she didn't get at home. She found their relationship so exciting that she began to think only of dates, partying with the "right crowd," and concerts.

Her grades nose-dived. Suddenly, Janelle was crash-studying and getting very little sleep. Even with a great deal of encouragement and support, Janelle could not get her life under control.

Options

Janelle could heroically make greater efforts to catch up on her school work and regulate her study, sleep, and social life, but she feels unable to do so. She could ask help from her parents and school staff, but instead she wants to try to do it herself. Like many other teens, she could cry for help by risking her life through a suicide attempt, or she could ask for shelter in a hospital setting for a time, where the environment is stable.

Choice

Janelle was unable to choose wisely, but at least she avoided the seriously risky options. To her credit, she chose to accept some time in an adolescent center where she worked hard with her family to turn around her deteriorating reactions.

Consequences

It will take some time, but Janelle and her family are committed to making everything right.

Consistency

Janelle's parents have a lot of work to do. First, they must straighten out their own

> marriage problems, being consistent in their love and interaction with each other before they can help Janelle. But their willingness to undergo counseling with their daughter is a wonderful step in the right direction.

The consistency of parents, school personnel, and counselors is vital in helping any adolescent or young adult gain and keep control in the topsy-turvy world of teens. Even when you get discouraged with the emotional storms and frustrations of parenting a teen, don't give up. You *can* make a difference in your teen's life!

RESPONSIBILITY

Dilemma #1

Deidre's mother died when she was nine. Her distraught father was busy with his professional life, but he spent time with his daughter. He also provided a housekeeper, who was a poor role model and allowed Deidre to be in charge of the house and herself without much direction or guidance. Lacking the security of appropriate boundaries created extreme willfulness in Deidre.

Her father, feeling sorry for the motherless girl, developed a pattern of lecturing and rescuing. When she was sixteen, he not only bought her a car, but a brand-new car. "Nothing is too good for my little girl!" her father had emphasized, trying to make up for Deidre's lack of a mother.

It didn't take long for Deidre to receive too many traffic violations. Soon she was responsible for an accident that totalled the car. Because of his contacts with the police department, her father rescued her from the consequences. He lectured her severely, then bought her another new car—this time a sports car.

Deidre's story doesn't end there. At seventeen, she developed a habit of selecting boyfriends who were objectionable to her father. "You just don't understand, Daddy!" was the response he received after one of his numerous lectures. Nothing was solved. Deidre continued to date the boys, and her father continued to lecture.

When Deidre was eighteen, she became pregnant. Her father was repulsed by the boy, who was a heavy drinker and seemed not to know where he was going in life. But Deidre was determined to marry him.

Shortly before the wedding, the boy was killed in a car accident, caused by his alcohol abuse. Deidre had the baby, but now she wanted a career. To make this possible for her, her father's new wife took care of Deidre's baby while Deidre went to secretarial college at her father's expense. Deidre was not expected to work for the tuition or to pay any of her living or childcare expenses.

Before completing the secretarial course, she dropped out, married, and immediately had another baby. At the age of twenty-five, Deidre tired of her husband and children and left them for another man.

Although her father disapproved strongly of her lifestyle and choices, he continued to finance them through the years and tried to cover up her pattern of disasters.

Let's put this story into the SOCCC framework.

Situation   Deidre was given a new car at 16. She was rescued from her numerous traffic citations by her father. She totaled the car and was immediately given another, better car. She consistently dated boys unacceptable to her father. He consistently lectured her. She became pregnant. The father's new wife took care of the baby while Deidre went to secretarial college, paid for by Dad, as were all her living expenses. She dropped out, married, had another child, then left her husband and children for another man. The father financed this relationship also.

Options   The father had an option of encouraging his daughter to work for what she wanted. He could have made her responsible for the consequences of her thoughtless behavior rather than rescuing and lecturing.

Or he could continue the pattern of rescuing and lecturing.

The daughter had options, too. She could have listened to her father's advice and heeded it. She had the option of learning from her mistakes.

Or she could go on in her thoughtless, careless, uncontrolled behavior and expect her dad to pick up after her.

Choice   The father chose to lecture and then rescue the girl from her mishaps, usually with money.

The girl chose not to listen, to go her own way, do her own thing, and know that "good ol' Dad" would bail her out.

Consequences   Deidre's choices affected others negatively. She "used" the housekeeper, she "used" the new wife, she "used and abused" her father and husband, and she neglected and abandoned her children.

Consistency   Unfortunately, the only area in which this father was consistent was in his rescuing and lecturing. He didn't realize that by giving his "little girl" everything he was really destroying her power to make good choices.

We can only wonder what would have happened to Deidre if her father had been a SOCCC parent and had allowed Deidre to assume the consequences of any of the situations that she faced along life's path rather than lecturing and rescuing.

What if there had been no money? Would Deidre have worked? And if she had worked to earn money, would she have been so careless with her schooling and with a car that she had bought? If she had assumed the responsibility for her choices, would she have shown respect to others? Would Deidre have learned to continue in a marriage and in motherhood even when it wasn't easy?

We can never know for certain, but we do know that Deidre's quest for immediate gratification with no regard for anyone else, including her own children, resulted from a lack of training in responsibility in her early years.

LIFESTYLE CHOICES

Dilemma #1

Glenn was brilliant—at least that's what his achievement tests indicated. But his grades were only average through high school, which was a disappointment to his SOCCC parents. When Glenn announced he was not planning to attend college, his parents were deeply grieved. "To think that someone with your potential for extraordinary academic success would not attend college is tragic," they lamented. "You've not done well only because you have chosen not to apply yourself, but we know you can do the work."

"I know I can do the work too," Glenn replied. "But, for right now, I'm just not interested—mainly because I don't know what I want to do."

His parents were irritated. "Just how do you plan on finding out what you want to do?" they inquired.

"I've thought a lot about it, and even though I know this will be hard for you to understand, please accept my decision." His parents listened intently. "I plan to work for a steamship company and travel around the world until I see enough and know enough to make a decent decision about the rest of my life."

His parents were stunned. They couldn't believe what they were hearing, and it was difficult to assimilate the ramifications of all he had told them.

"Don't say anything right now," Glenn requested. "Think about it, talk about it, and try to see it from my viewpoint. I don't know what I want to do, and I do know I want to see the world, and this is a way to do it."

His parents did think and talk about it. In fact, they spoke of little else for days, viewing the decision from every angle. They came to the conclusion that their son had done nothing wrong in choosing not to go to college, and that perhaps Glenn's wanderlust was just a postponement. They gave their approval, and a farewell family celebration was held in Glenn's honor.

For over a year, Glenn traveled everywhere, faithfully communicating by letter and by telephone. His parents appreciated being kept informed, and they felt content with the shipboard work he was doing. He was certainly seeing the world and learning much about people and places.

At long last, the call they'd been waiting for came. "I'm coming *home!*" Glenn said with enthusiasm. "I've given notice to the steamship company, and I'll see you at the end of the month." His parents looked forward to the family reunion with great anticipation.

Glenn had been thinking about what to do with the rest of his life. During that time away, he had decided that the best way he could utilize his abilities and help needy people was to study anthropology and pursue a career in Third-World development. "I have seen so much hunger and poverty around the world," he said. "I'd like to have a small part in relieving the misery of people. I want your approval.

I hope I have it because I'll need a lot of support in the years ahead."

His parents were elated. Their fondest dreams concerning Glenn were going to come true, and all it took was time, patience, and understanding.

Situation	Glenn was an average student of high ability who did not know what he wanted to do professionally.
Options	Glenn could have given his parents immediate gratification by attending college. He also had the option of working, seeing the world, and slowly making a decision of how he wanted to spend the rest of his life.
	His parents had the option of creating enormous pressure on Glenn to attend college or incur their wrath. They also had the option of respecting his decision and encouraging him, although his plan did not coincide with theirs.
Choice	Glenn made a choice to work for a steamship company and see the world, while deciding what he wanted to do with the rest of his life.
	His parents made a choice to support him in his decision and not exert pressure on him to do what they wanted.
Consequences	Glenn had an opportunity to see the world, to witness the physical misery of

people everywhere, and to make a career decision.

Glenn's parents saw their lifelong dream coming true.

Consistency   The parents knew what they wanted for their son—a college education. But, more importantly, they wanted him to be a responsible individual, so they graciously accepted his very difficult decision and were rewarded with continuing communication and the maturity of his professional choice.

Whatever the age or stage of your children, the SOCCC system will work when it's used with gentle strength and love.

Tips for Parents

How you act or react as a parent can make all the difference in the world to your child. We know that parenting is not always easy. Frequently, situations will come up that test your patience level, your endurance, and your emotional stability. Before you react to each situation, take a deep breath. This gives you a moment to cool off and time to think. Keep in mind your options and choose wisely. Here are some things to remember that will help you as you develop your parenting skills:

- Instead of reacting emotionally or impulsively, *assess the situation clearly.*

- Instead of repeating only one option (which may not be working well), *consider all the options available.*

- Instead of allowing anger or helplessness to control you, *choose your course wisely and plan carefully.*

- Instead of repeating needless mistakes out of old habits, *review the consequences* of your choices and learn from both your successes and mistakes.

- In all you do, *be consistent* but not rigid.

Learning this process, practicing it, and teaching it to your children will keep harmony in your home now and help assure a successful outcome for your children in the future.

– 14 –
The
C
SOCC
Send-Off

Everyone, sooner or later, sits down
to his banquet of consequences.
ROBERT LOUIS STEVENSON

Jack was so excited! It was the day of his very first big race. He proudly put on his fastest racing shoes and, with a big grin on his five-year-old face, joined the other children at the starting line. Sizing up the others in the race, Jack's mom and dad thought he had a pretty good chance of coming in at least second or third, maybe even first!

The booming command came over the loud speaker, "Get on your mark, Get ready, Get set . . . GO!" All the children dashed off at break-neck speed. Jack got off to a head start, ran well, but then—something went wrong.

What was it? His mom and dad looked at each other with great concern. Jack was slowing down. Then he looked back at his parents with tears in his eyes. Could it be a sudden illness? Perhaps a piercing pain?

The other children were nearing the finish line as an embarrassed, tearful Jack hobbled to his parents. They comforted him, then gently asked, "What's wrong?" They wanted to know what could have happened to cause him to give up the race he'd anticipated for days.

"I-I didn't know wh-where I-I w-w-was go-going," he stammered, still whimpering. His parents stifled a smile, assured him it was O.K., that he had started off great, and that next time he'd find out exactly where the goal was ahead of time.

Long- and Short-Term Goals

It's all too easy for us as parents to become like Jack. We look forward to becoming parents, and we're thrilled when a child is born. Then we begin the awesome task of parenting, working day by day, but do we know where we are heading? Do we consciously work toward long-term goals for our children as well as immediate and short-term goals? And do these goals complement each other?

Without clear goals, we cannot guide our children to make wise decisions. Without making wise decisions, our children will not reach their full potential.

The SOCCC parent has a headstart on goal-setting because both long-term child-rearing goals and short-term goals are contained in the essence of the SOCCC approach. Let's take a look at them.

1. The parent makes a commitment to consistency.

2. The parent provides the child with limited, age-appropriate choices.

3. The parent allows the child to make his or her own decision from the choices provided, unless there is serious risk involved.

4. The parent permits the child to assume the responsibility for the consequences of the choice, teaching how to prevent future mistakes.

5. Being allowed the opportunity to make choices and reap the consequences from the earliest age, the child learns how to make responsible choices, learns to accept the consequences of each choice, and learns to make increasingly better choices as a result.

Dr. James Dobson, the eminent psychologist whose daily broadcast is heard over hundreds of radio stations and whose child-rearing books have sold millions says, "The parental purpose should be to grant increasing freedom and responsibility year by year, so that when the child gets beyond adult control, he will no longer need it."[1] Dr. Dobson has diagrammed this "Orderly Transfer of Freedom and Responsibility" that prepares the child each year for the moment of full independence. It looks like this:[2]

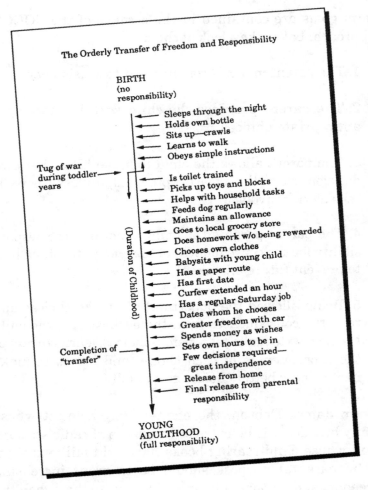

The Orderly Transfer of Freedom and Responsibility

BIRTH
(no responsibility)

Tug of war during toddler years

- Sleeps through the night
- Holds own bottle
- Sits up—crawls
- Learns to walk
- Obeys simple instructions
- Is toilet trained
- Picks up toys and blocks
- Helps with household tasks
- Feeds dog regularly
- Maintains an allowance
- Goes to local grocery store
- Does homework w/o being rewarded
- Chooses own clothes
- Babysits with young child
- Has a paper route
- Has first date
- Curfew extended an hour
- Has a regular Saturday job
- Dates whom he chooses
- Greater freedom with car
- Spends money as wishes
- Sets own hours to be in
- Few decisions required—great independence
- Release from home
- Final release from parental responsibility

(Duration of Childhood)

Completion of "transfer"

YOUNG ADULTHOOD
(full responsibility)

We know you can be a SOCCC parent! And if you have not begun, we encourage you to start today. The SOCCC approach to parenting will instill qualities in your children that will give them incredible resources to become responsible, dependable adults who will make positive contributions to society, demonstrate lifelong self-control, and have the courage to think objectively and say "No!" when confronted with unhealthy peer group pressure at any age.

This beautiful old poem poignantly expresses the crucial opportunity and responsibility of parenthood.

I took a piece of plastic clay
And idly fashioned it one day
And as my fingers pressed it still,
It moved and yielded to my will.

I came again when days were past;
The bit of clay was hard at last.
The form I gave it still it bore,
But I could change that form no more.

I took a piece of living clay
And gently formed it day by day,
And molded with God's power and art
A young child's soft and yielding heart.

I came again when years were gone;
A man now I looked upon,
And he that early impress wore,
And I could change him never more.
—Arthur Guiterman

As soon as you begin to use the SOCCC parenting approach, we know that you will see the positive results in your home. Every moment that you spend in providing your child with limited, age-appropriate choices and in permitting your child to assume the responsibility for the consequences of those choices, will be rewarded. Your child will grow in confidence, in self-respect, and in respect for you. As you and your child learn together, you will witness growing maturity as your child makes increasingly better choices through the coming years. What a wonderful opportunity you have as parents! And there isn't a better time to start than right now.

For every choice in life, there is a	**C** onsequence.
The child assumes responsibility for his choices and learns	**H** ow to make wise decisions and prevent future mistakes.
The child is given more	**O** ptions and greater opportunities
to make	**I** ncreasingly complex choices.
The parent is committed to	**C** onsistency
from	**E** arly childhood through young adulthood.
For the betterment of home and society, let's	**S** OCCC it to 'em through the years.

Why? Because . . .

Choices Are NOT Child's Play!

Notes

Introduction
1. Sidney Sheldon, *Rage of Angels* (New York: William Morrow, 1980), p. 504.

Chapter One
1. Glenn, Stephen H., and Jane Nelsen, Ed.D., *Raising Self-Reliant Children in a Self-Indulgent World* (Rocklin, Calif.: Prima Publishing and Communications, 1989), pp. 30-31.
2. "Getting Tough," a study conducted by the Fullerton, California Police Department and the California Department of Education, in *Time*, February 1, 1988, p. 54.
3. Gesell, Arnold, M.D., Frances L. Ilg, M.D., and Louise B. Ames, M.D., *Youth: The Years from Ten to Sixteen* (New York: Harper & Row, 1956), p. 131.
4. Calhoun, John A., "Violence, Youth, and a Way Out" in *Children Today*, 17:19-21.
5. U.S. Department of Education, *What Works: Schools without Drugs* (1989), pp. 2-12.
6. Ibid.
7. U.S. Department of Health and Human Services, *NIDA Capsules*, August, 1988.

Chapter Two
1. Glasser, William, M.D., *Reality Therapy* (New York: Harper & Row, 1965).
2. Kanner, Leo, M.D., *Textbook of Child Psychoanalysis,* n.d., n.p.
3. Berne, Dr. Eric Berne, *Games People Play* (New York: Grove Press, 1964).

Chapter Five
1. Canter, Lee, and Lee Hausner, Ph.D., *Homework without Tears* (New York: Harper & Row, 1987), p. 3.

Chapter Seven
1. Glenn, p. 104.

Chapter Eight
1. U.S. Department of Education, *What Works: Research About Teaching and Learning* (1986), pp. 40-45.
2. Maxwell, John C., *Your Attitude: Key to Success* (San Bernardino, Calif.: Here's Life Publishers, 1984).
3. Nelson, Jane, Ed.D., *Positive Discipline* (New York: Ballantine Books, 1987), pp. 72-74.
4. Holt, Pat, and Grace Ketterman, M.D., *When You Feel Like Screaming* (Wheaton, Ill.: Harold Shaw Publishers, 1988).

Chapter Nine
1. Maxwell, Dr. John C., *How to Grow a Leader* (Bonita, Calif.: Injoy Life Club, ,1985), Vol. 4, 111, Side B.
2. Waitley, Denis, *Seeds of Greatness* (Old Tappan, N.J.: Fleming H. Revell, 1983), pp. 72-74.

Chapter Twelve
1. Elkind, Dr. David, *The Hurried Child* (Reading, Mass.: Addison-Wesley Publishing Company, 1981).